Digital Imaging:

a practical handbook

Digital ...
...handbook

Digital Imaging:
a practical handbook

Stuart D Lee

NEAL-SCHUMAN PUBLISHERS, INC.
NEW YORK
IN ASSOCIATION WITH
LIBRARY ASSOCIATION PUBLISHING
LONDON

Published by
Neal-Schuman Publishers, Inc.
100 Varick Street
New York, NY 10013

© Stuart D Lee 2001

Library of Congress Cataloging-in-Publication Data
Lee, Stuart D.
    Digital imaging : a practical handbook / Stuart D. Lee.
       p. cm.
    ISBN 1-55570-405-0 (alk. paper)
    1. Digital preservation--Handbooks, manuals, etc. 2. Library materials--Conservation and restoration--Handbooks, manuals, etc. I. Title.

Z681.3.D53 L44 2000
025.8'4'0285--dc21   00-045075

ISBN 1-55570-405-0

Published simultaneously with Library Association Publishing, London.
Printed and made in Great Britain.

Contents

Acknowledgments

This book is a result of several previous enterprises and thus thanks should be offered to those people who have helped me in my work on previous occasions. Most notably this refers to the Wilfred Owen Project which could not have been completed without the work done by Paul Groves, and the initial faith placed in the project by Tom Franklin. Following on, many of the recommendations made here are based on the experiences of the Andrew W Mellon Foundation funded project at Oxford to scope the University's digital collections. Once again I would like to offer thanks to the Director of University Library Services, Reg Carr, for providing me with the opportunity to undertake the study and the project's Steering Committee for all their numerous contributions.

Numerous people have contributed to the content of this book both directly and indirectly, and I would like to take this opportunity to acknowledge their support: Neil Beagrie, Lou Burnard, Steve Chapman, David Cooper, Matthew Dovey, Nancy Elkington, Eileen Fenton, Mike Fraser, Richard Gartner, Anne Kenney, Peter Kidd, Alan Morrison, Michael Popham, John Price-Wilkin, Alex Reid, Oya Rieger, Mark Sandler, Julius Smit, McKenzie Smith, and Karla Youngs. Thanks should also go to: Andrew Colleran, Paul Conway, Skip Cox, Clive Field, Robyn Grimes, Bill Hall, Peter Hirtle, Oliver Habicht, Phillip Hunter, David Inglis, Susan Jephcott, Bill Jupp, Patricia Killiard, Alan Lock, Brain McKenna, Adrienne Muir, Charles Oppenheim, Chris Powell, Geoff Smith, Oliver Vicars-Harris, Ellis Weinberger and Alicia Wise.

My main thanks must go to Sarah Porter for taking the time to read through the document and to provide numerous helpful comments and corrections.

Introduction

The aim of the book is to provide practical guidance for anyone who is about to embark on a digitization project or is interested in this growth area. In particular, those charged with initiating digitization projects, such as senior librarians and managers, will find that the book adopts a practical approach to decision-making, following the life-cycle of the digitization project from inception to completion. It follows the process of digitizing, from initial inception through the capture, delivering and archiving stages, outlining workflows and discussing relevant issues along the way. It looks at how one captures from print, photographs, surrogates, and other material – covering the digitization of rare and fragile material as well as the bulk digitization of grey material. The book will outline the reasons why digitization is so popular at the moment, and what advantages and disadvantages it presents.

A book of this kind comes at an opportune moment in the development of the new technologies. Clearly the digitization of cultural heritage material is commanding considerable popularity internationally, notably at government level. Whilst the US has its National Digital Library Program (led by the Library of Congress), Europe is working on a variety of Telematics projects funded by the EC, and Australia is working on the Co-Operative Digitization Project. More interestingly, there is common consent globally on the perceived advantages this may offer at a cultural level. As the United Kingdom's New Opportunity Fund (NOF) states, the emerging technologies (particularly digital imaging) present:

. . . an **opportunity** to make the **resources** of the libraries, archives, museums, galleries, education sectors and a wide **range** of other organisations more **accessible** (p.10)   (**http://www.nof-digitise.org/**)

This accurately reflects the vision behind the Library of Congress's digitization plan; aiming to be:

. . . an extension to every desktop, classroom, and personal library. Patterns of use of the World Wide Web already demonstrate that teachers, scholars, and students will want to refer to items in the digital realm as active links from reading lists, articles, textbooks, and term papers.

(**http://memory.loc.gov/ammem/dli2/html/lcndlp.html#Vision**)

This in turn mirrors Government policy in the US. President Clinton has spoken at length on bridging the 'digital divide', because, as he sees it:

In the new century, innovations in science and technology will be key not only to the health of the environment, but to miraculous improvements in the quality of our lives and advances in the economy.

President Bill Clinton, January 27, 2000

(**http://www.whitehouse.gov/WH/Accomplishments/
technology.html**)

Earlier, in October 1997, heralding the launch of the National Grid for Learning (NGfL), the Prime Minister of the United Kingdom Tony Blair stated:

Technology has revolutionised the way we work and is now set to transform education. Children cannot be effective in tomorrow's world if they are trained in yesterday's skills. Nor should teachers be denied the tools that other professionals take for granted. The Grid [National Grid for Learning] will be a way of finding and using on-line learning and teaching materials. It will help users to find their way around the wealth of content available over the Internet.

'Connecting the learning society'

(**http://www.dfee.gov.uk/grid/foreword.htm**)

The global picture is discussed more fully in Appendix A, but for the moment it is worth bearing the above declarations in mind. They clearly demonstrate that there is considerable political will behind harnessing the new technologies to increase access to resources that can further the educational experiences of everyone – be they academics, students, schoolteachers, children or the general public. To succeed in this the resources held by the museums, libraries and galleries need to be available in digital form so that they can be distributed more easily, most notably through the international medium of the Internet. It is understandable, therefore, that much of the new money available is going into the development of large bodies of electronic content. One aspect of this (and it is by no means the whole story, as we shall see in later chapters) is the process of digitization.

As with most top-down initiatives, the pressure has fallen on the people already overworked as it is – in this case the holders of the items, or the subject specialists – to carry this digitization forward. Furthermore, under present financial conditions, the temptation is indeed great to try get a slice of the digitization pie. The advantages of digitization are explored in Chapter 1, but for now, if one were to take a purely mercenary approach, it is clear that any offer of funding, especially when dealing with the types of figures quoted by national funding bodies, has to be explored by institutions that are already under-resourced.

The most succinct description of the problems and opportunities presented by these new technologies was outlined in a short discussion outlining the impetus behind the JSTOR initiative, based in the US. Here they noted:

> The movement toward the use of electronic technologies has introduced new challenges for libraries and library staff. Retraining the traditional librarian to accept the new technologies and provide reference services for the electronic materials has been one such challenge that appears to have been largely overcome. Almost all major libraries now have computer equipment (although never enough!) and are connected to a network that allows users to gain access to electronic products, services and databases.
>
> But the increasing availability of electronic technologies introduces problems that have not yet been solved. Librarians worry about who is going

to be responsible for archiving the electronic materials and insuring that important scholarly publications are available to tomorrow's researchers. They are also concerned that they will be required to understand and provide support for thousands of different electronic interfaces. Finally, they want technologies on the usage of scholarly materials.

JSTOR: The Need (**http://www.jstor.ac.uk/about/need.html**)

The book fills a clear gap in the market. The recent publication by Kenney and Rieger (2000) offers an advanced study of current digitization issues, but is clearly aimed at existing practitioners in the field. At the other extreme, introductory guides for beginners tend to be cursory, incomplete, ephemeral, and dispersed. What is needed, then, is a book for librarians, project managers, or students who are coming to this area as relative beginners. They will want to know what the main questions and issues surrounding digital imaging are at present, and to get a realistic overview of a project from its beginning to the final delivery.

As with any publication of this size, the coverage has had to be selective. Therefore certain elements have had to be covered in a rather cursory fashion, leaving readers to turn to more elaborate studies. To assist in this the book concludes with a series of references to allow readers to take their study further.

The process of digitization is littered with many pitfalls, traps and abandoned projects. This book aims to act as a guide through the hazards of digitizing images. Rather than focusing only on the technical side of capturing images, this handbook will take the reader through the various stages of a digital project, pointing out the questions that need to be asked at each point, and offering advice and suggestions to make the management and eventual delivery as painless as possible.

Stuart Lee

1 | Where do you start? The digitization project

Introduction

This chapter will look at some of the basic questions and definitions underlining the term digitization and the digital project. Before commencing, however, it may be worthwhile describing a typical (but hypothetical) scenario that illustrates digitization from start to finish.

Example: Victorian diaries

A large library reacting to an external funding initiative has decided to enter into the world of digitization. It begins by selecting several items from its own collections – in this case a group of diaries from a well-known Victorian painter – with the aim of making digital facsimiles available over the Internet. Each item is originally 'passed' by the resident conservation expert as being able to withstand the capturing process, and is then moved to the studio. Using a digital camera, images are taken from each page of the diaries and archived on the computing system. The individual images are then catalogued, edited as appropriate, and presented to the world on a freely available website.

This example is surprisingly typical of many digitization projects. In terms of content it can be seen to be concentrating on paper-based material that is out of copyright, but also on items that are rare or unique. As is the norm nowadays, the resulting archive will be delivered via the world wide web. More importantly, it follows a traditional life-cycle of:

- the selection of the material to go into the project
- the digitization of the material
- the delivery of the material.

Furthermore, even given this sketchy overview, one could begin to visualize the staff (or services) that would be needed to complete the project:

- an expert to select the items
- a conservation advisor to agree to the digitization
- a digital photographer
- a cataloguer
- a technical expert to mount and maintain the website.

If we were to see ourselves as the managers of this project, we could summarize the questions we have already asked (and produced answers to) as:

- Why?
- What?
- How?

In other words:

- Why is the material being digitized?
- What material is being captured?
- How will the aims of the project be fulfilled?

Successfully answering these three questions from the outset of each project will greatly increase one's chances of completion.

In essence, this book will follow these three essential questions in order, so as best to reflect the real life-cycle of a digitization project. That is to say, one needs to be clear as to why the digitization is happening in the first place and what exactly will be captured. This in turn will allow one to consider the technical solutions needed to complete the project.

It is clear that these questions should be seen only as main headings of investigation. In reality they each contain a multitude of issues and further questions that need to be raised. Furthermore, everyone who has gone through such a project will state that it is undeniably an iterative process – ie answers to questions asked later will force one to reassess some of the decisions made at the beginning – and more worryingly it is a process with a seemingly random timescale. Many previous discussions of digitization projects (and the management thereof) imply that all the information one needs to answer any questions or address any problem is accurate and readily to hand, and that there is always a reasonable amount of time to assess issues fully and to come up with the correct solution. This, it has to be said, is rarely the case. Most of the time, one is forced to work under considerable pressure in terms of time and finance, striving to meet a schedule of increasingly unrealistic deliverables. One is forced to make snap decisions, or offer best-guess solutions. If, after reading this book, *you* find that this is true for *your* project then you should realize that there is nothing unusual in this – it happens with most projects – but in order to increase the chances that the decisions made are the best ones, one should become familiar with the issues raised in this handbook. To begin with, however, there is a core question that needs to be answered.

What is digitization?

Digitization is the conversion of an analog signal or code into a digital signal or code. Most of our everyday life is spent in the analog world, receiving natural signals. Our eyes take in colours, our ears pitch and tone, delivered to them in waveforms. The digital world cannot deal with these continually changing patterns and needs to get the information into a medium which computers can handle. It does this by sampling the analog patterns and converting them to simple numerical values, in this case ones and zeros, or *bits* as they are often called. It is for this reason that people often use terms like 'conversion' or 'capture' as synonyms for digitization – ie the analog signal is *converted* to a digital one, or the analog is *captured* into digital form.

The detailed technical aspects of how this process takes place should not concern most people, but managers and students of digital projects will need to verse themselves in some of the issues surrounding resolutions and file sizes, discussed in full in Chapter 3. For now, though, it is enough to accept that the technology is readily available in the form of cameras and other capture devices (eg scanners) that allow one to convert analog images into digital images – ie they can be *digitized*.

Why do we digitize material?

Having accepted that established technologies exist to convert the analog to the digital, it is worthwhile continuing our interrogation by asking why it is that so many institutions wish to do this. Gould and Ebdon (1999) noted that nearly two-thirds of the libraries they surveyed had a digitization research programme in operation, the majority having started as far back as 1995–96. But what made them embark on this? For now, the main reasons why libraries, museums, publishers, and so on undertake digitization projects are in order to:

- increase access (or sales)
- preserve the original.

Increasing access

The most quoted and easily defended advantage offered by digitization is that it can increase access to particular resources. In most cases, items that are selected for conversion are rare or unique, usually housed in only a handful of locations world-wide. The physical item therefore has limited access (one actually has to go to the item to view it, or go through a reprographics unit to order a surrogate). Furthermore, reflecting the standing of the institution and the rare quality of its resources, physical access to the item may even be limited. For example, a member of the public cannot simply walk into the manuscript room in the Library of Congress and request to see any item he or she wishes. Many figures can be quoted to confirm this assumption, but perhaps the most striking is that offered by the British Library (**http://www.bl.uk**). In 1999 they recorded figures of 407,000 readers visiting the library to look at its holdings, but a staggering ten million looked at their website and the online collections during the same period.

Digitization can tackle this problem by creating an accurate facsimile of the original item (or more properly a numerical description of the originals – see Chapter 3). If a digital facsimile of an illustration is created, for example, it can be converted very quickly to a format suitable for the Internet (most notably for the web). Assuming that there are no restrictions in place, a reasonably high-quality image can be made available to millions of users, who can all look at the item simultaneously, from anywhere in the world and at any time of the global day. Thus a process of democratization begins, as this image will not be restricted to researchers or curators but can be viewed by people from any background (from schoolchildren to commercial employees). Furthermore, because the item is being stored as a series of bits, theory states that it is possible to copy from the original code ad infinitum without any degradation. One is simply copying across a series of zeros and ones, as opposed to converting an analog record to another analog record (which will undoubtedly involve a loss of quality).

The above statements are supported by all manner of studies. Tamara Swora (1996) in a discussion of why material is selected for digital 'reformatting' argued that the overriding issue had to be to increase access to the collection. This was reinforced by the conclusions reached by the Focus Group, attached to the Library and Information Commission which met in October 1997 to look at selection criteria for digitization. They decided that:

- improving access was the main priority for digitization
- the main criterion for selecting a resource was its uniqueness.

Preserving the original

A more contentious issue relates to preservation. Strong advocates of digitization propose that, if one captures an original into digital form at extremely high quality, then that file can act as a preservation copy in a similar fashion to a microfilm master. However, putting aside the argument as to whether any copy (be it film or digital) can be viewed as 'preservation', the counter-argument to this relates to the questionable longevity of a digital file. Although one can safely assume that under adequate conditions the bit stream (ie the ones and zeros that make up the file) can be preserved, it is highly debatable, even with the most elaborate of migration systems in place, whether we can be certain that the file will be usable 10 or 20 years hence. The end of the 1990s, for example, witnessed the growing problem of files created in the earlier part of the decade being no longer readable or viewable under current operating systems. Although solutions are being developed to counteract this problem, the digital object as a preservation copy still compares unfavourably with microfilm, which under correct conditions will be readable (using very limited technology) in hundreds of years.

There is one area where we can affirm that digitization assists in preservation – namely in deflecting demand away from handling the original (sometimes known as 'rescue digitization'). The theory is that the availability of high quality digital surrogates will satisfy most users' demands and therefore reduce the need to look at, and handle, the source item itself. Furthermore, as digital files can be endlessly copied without any sign of degradation (once there is a high-quality electronic master), the burden on the often overworked reprographic unit can be alleviated. Copying a digital file can only take a matter of seconds, and using correct software it can be easily printed out to photographic quality. However, there are problems with this. Wider access brings wider knowledge of the existence of the item, and as has been found with microfilming and online catalogues, this leads to more researchers requesting to see the item. Ironically, then, the availability of digital surrogates can in fact have the effect of increasing the number of accesses to the original. The only way this can be deterred is either by introducing strong institutional policies that prohibit access once a high-quality digital surrogate is available, and/or by having sufficient hardware and software available in reading rooms to allow users to perform their research to a satisfactory level on the electronic copy.

The cost effectiveness of digitization

Regardless of one's views on digital preservation and the problems of increased access, one of the hard facts of digitization that needs to be confronted early on is that it is extremely expensive to undertake. The unit cost of digitizing will be discussed in Chapter 4, but for now a simple checklist illustrates how quickly costs can mount up. To 'digitize' material requires hardware, software, a delivery and cataloguing system, and staffing. Taken together these can quickly amount to a substantial sum of money. Even looking at the unit cost of an image, once it has been prepared, digitized, post-edited, catalogued and delivered, the 'real' cost may amount to upwards of £15–£20 per picture. Multiplied by the number of items one often comes across in archives and libraries, then even the smallest collection can amount to several thousands of pounds. How then can it ever be cost-effective to digitize?

The reply to this rests on the idea of spreading costs. Although one is often dealing with large amounts of money, one is also looking at a potentially much higher number of accesses. An image may cost £20 in total to capture, but this may seem highly cost-effective if it receives 10,000 'hits' (or viewings) a month. The issue of cost-effectiveness, then, like so many topics that will be discussed in this book, is a double-edged sword. There are clear advantages and disadvantages that can be easily outlined, but unfortunately at the same time there are a seemingly equal number of grey areas. Undoubtedly this reflects the fact that we are only just beginning to understand the issues fully and to answer some of the questions that surround digitization.

The digitization project life-cycle

This chapter began with a fictitious example of how a digitization project might proceed with diaries from the Victorian period. However, this process first needs to be described even more clearly by an initial attempt at defining the life-cycle of a digitization project. Robinson (1993) established the term *digitization chain* as a way of looking at the processes involved in converting an analog source to a digital copy. Now, thanks to the experience gained in the last seven years, it is more advisable to view the conversion process as part of a much larger initiative, and to look instead at the *digitization project life-cycle* (see Beagrie and Greenstein, 1998). An overview of this is given in Figure 1.1.

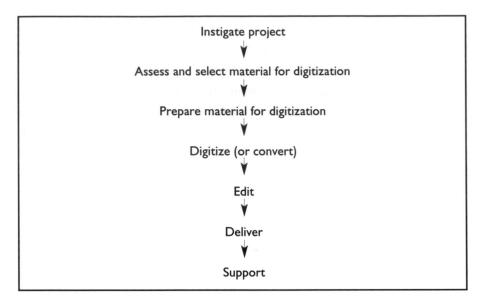

Instigate project

↓

Assess and select material for digitization

↓

Prepare material for digitization

↓

Digitize (or convert)

↓

Edit

↓

Deliver

↓

Support

Fig. 1.1   *Overview of the digitization project life-cycle*

To explain this more completely: at some point the project will be agreed (which could range from a single image to a complete archive). The material that is to go into the digital collection will be assessed by a variety of experts, and items will be selected from this for digitization (see Chapter 2). These in turn will be prepared, and then digitized or scanned (Chapters 3 and 4). The digital files will be edited as appropriate to the project's aims, and then delivered to the target audience (Chapter 5), eg via the web. In addition some IT support will have to be offered to ensure that continued access is maintained.

In our opening example of the Victorian diaries, a preliminary list was given of the staff – or more correctly the services – that would be needed to complete the project. Expanding this, using the above life-cycle, it could be stated that the full digitization project would need access to the following:

- subject experts
- conservation experts
- digital and film photographers
- cataloguers
- IT specialists

- management
- administration.

Throughout the project each of the personnel will be called upon for input at several stages, and decisions will have to be made by them in their own areas of expertise, with someone being ultimately responsible for the overall management of the project. The rest of this book describes the project life-cycle through its various stages, at each point asking the appropriate questions, raising any problematic issues and providing some suggested solutions. In the light of this it is worth considering Simon Tanner's observation (Tanner, 2000) which will prepare the reader well for the subsequent discussions:

> Digitisation is a tool and not a purpose all in itself. Digitisation is not solely about technology, but more importantly it is about successfully achieving information goals and needs.

Chapter summary

The 1990s was the decade of digitization and the 2000s show signs of continuing this trend. At the end of this book in Appendix C there is a list of some of the most important sites and projects that have been involved in digitization over the past ten years. It is recommended that these are followed to see what type of material has been covered, and by whom.

The above sections introduced some of the basic concepts of digitization. Having read this outline you should now be familiar with:

- the term 'digitization'
- the fundamental questions every digitization project needs to address
- the main advantages and disadvantages of digitizing material
- the life-cycle of the digitization project.

2 | What are you digitizing? Instigation, selection and assessment

Introduction

Chapter 1 explained some of the issues at the foundation of any digitization project, ending with a summary of the full life-cycle of a digitization project. This chapter progresses the discussion by looking at the first two stages of the project: namely its instigation, and the subsequent assessment and selection of material. To begin with, asking the question how and why does a digitization project actually start?

Instigation of the project

Most projects begin as an idea. This may stem from a new funding opportunity, or it may be part of the institution's overall strategy in managing its collections. For example, the funding councils may suddenly announce new money for the digitization of resources applicable to regional history, at which point one will need to select items from collections that match the target area. Alternatively, a library may be actively involved in digitizing all of its rare and fragile material in an attempt to reduce handling of the original. Again one will need to go through the collections and pick out items which would benefit from this rescue digitization.

Yet even the beginning of a project can be more complicated than would appear at first glance. The conditions under which the project is instigated will directly influence one's ability to control all subsequent processes.

First, one could define any response to an external request as *reactive digitization*. Within this definition, it is clear that there are levels of 'reaction', and indeed levels of control one has over the way the digitization will develop. If, for example, the funding from the external source is aimed at general digitization (ie non-specific targets), then one can select at will. More often than not, though, the funding will be more restricted, stating that the money should go to digitizing material in a certain subject area or genre (and this is as true for commercial companies as it is for non-profit organizations). Again, however, although one is working under increased constraints this time, there is still a level of control over which items would be selected. At the extreme, however, is what is termed 'on-demand digitization' or 'ad hoc digitization', whereby users or customers can request individual items to be digitized and pay the cost for the conversion and delivery (in a library setting this is the digital equivalent or add-on to a standard reprographics service). Again this could be considered 'reactive' as the project is responding to an external request, yet the control over the selection procedure has been almost entirely devolved into the hands of the end-user, and one may simply have to decide whether the item can undergo digitization or not (eg can it stand up to the wear and tear of the capture?), and if so when and where the digitization will take place.

On the other hand, *proactive digitization* takes place when the governing body targets particular collections of its own accord. Here the institution itself may have initiated the digital conversion programme of its collections – possibly for preservation reasons, more probably to increase access, but occasionally as a move to generate income (eg by selling the digital images). In this mode of operation one is in total control of the digitization programme, being at liberty to select any item from the collections, and digitize them in any order. The main problem facing many institutions, however, would be to get an accurate picture of the number of items at their disposal that could be targeted.

Even more problematic is moulding any digitization programme to user needs. More often than not, librarians, publishers or curators will have a good idea of the main collections under their care, but when offered the chance to digitize them they will immediately tend to focus on rare or unique items – in other words, material which is considered a 'treasure' by the institution. This may not necessarily reflect demand from users. For example, at a university the academics may require material for teaching to be made more accessible: this may not necessarily be items that are valuable in their own right, but instead frequently read articles or chapters in books. To accommodate both parties it is suggested that, prior to instigating any major proactive initiative in the digitization arena, as many people as possible in your institution are consulted (most easily by circulating a questionnaire). This would serve two purposes:

- to get an idea of the level of digitization expertise in your institution (eg individuals may have already undertaken small projects which you were unaware of)
- to produce a list of possible collections identified by academics, librarians and curators (as appropriate).

To assist in this a set of sample questionnaires is provided in Appendix B. In Chapter 5, the issue of how these could be used in an institution-wise initiative is explained, but for now it is worth noting the kinds of questions one might wish to ask. Primarily one is interested in the nature of any existing digitization project; but in terms of new collections one would also want to receive some preliminary details about the potential source material.

In reality, many institutions (notably libraries) operate in a reactive fashion when it comes to digitization, responding to any new call or opportunity for sponsorship. It is rare that an institution can attract money without any restrictions being attached, or find enough money from its own sources to be completely in control of their digitization. Nevertheless, that should not detract from moves to begin to assess and select your collections. A library that has a ready-to-hand prioritized list of collections it wishes to digitize is ready to respond quickly to new funding opportunities or to attract new sponsorship.

Whether a project will go ahead, and who makes this crucial decision, will rest upon several factors that will be investigated later. All that can be safely stated is that these decisions will often involve several parties, all providing essential input, including subject experts ('Is the project appropriate?'), conservation experts ('Is it safe?'), digitization staff ('Is it possible?') and managers ('Is it advisable?'). Furthermore it should be recognized that further through the life-cycle, problems may arise that in an extreme case could lead to the project being dropped. This instigation stage, therefore, should only be seen as the preliminary go-ahead.

Overall, one can state that it is extremely advantageous if an institution can be said to be in a position to:

- respond to new opportunities
- select appropriate items to meet user demands
- minimize the risk of making incorrect decisions at this early stage that will be time-consuming and costly to rectify later.

Therefore it is recommended that, once a project is given the *initial* go-ahead, the next stage that needs to be conducted is the assessment of the collection involved, in order to prioritize and select items from it.

Assessing projects and selecting material

Whatever the reasons behind the instigation of the project, one will, at quite an early stage, need to perform an initial assessment of the material under consideration and select the items from this that could be digitized. As Hazen et al (1998) note:

> The process of deciding what to digitize anticipates all the major stages of project implementation.

The scale of this and the questions one will need to ask will vary from case to case. For example, one may be assessing, selecting and prioritizing items from all of the collections in the institution. On the other hand, if one is working reactively and responding to external funding or reader requests, the selection strategy may be limited. Nevertheless, the criteria one uses to judge items need exploring and defining so that by the end of this stage of the digitization project life-cycle one is in a position to state:

- which items have been selected for digitization and why
- what demands or strategies will be met by digitizing them

- which digitization projects are of a higher priority than others.

As TASI (UK's Technical Advisory Service for Images note in their excellent guidelines for digital imaging (**http://www.tasi.ac.uk**):

> The first stage in any digital imaging project is to decide which items are going to be captured and prepare them for digitization. Questions that need to be asked include: 'Is the copyright situation clear?'; 'Do I have adequate information about the image to ensure retrieval?'; 'How are the images to be used and by whom?'; and 'What different image types or image modalities do I have in my collection?'.
>
> (*Image handling and preparation summary*, available at
> **http://www.tasi.ac.uk/building/image_hand_prep.html**)

Cherry-picking

A very common problem encountered when attempting to assess and select from collections is that of focusing on prized items from within the chosen archive. This is often termed 'cherry-picking'. A typical example of this would be the digitization of a rare manuscript of x-hundred folios of which only one or two leaves are ever consulted. Bearing in mind the high costs of digitization, when assessing the manuscript one could easily elect to digitize only the high-demand folios. Conversely, one could state that it should always be policy to digitize an item in its entirety, in this case the whole manuscript, as the mere availability of the other folios could lead to a rise in demand for them (through increased awareness). In general, however, there will be three possible solutions:

1 Yes, cherry-picking is acceptable as there is no point in digitizing items which no one will consult (or has consulted up to now). The spare capacity released by selective digitization of items in a collection can be redeployed to digitizing items elsewhere.

2 Yes, cherry-picking is acceptable but only as a last resort. Thereafter the possibilities of the project creating a revenue stream which can be directed

solely to digitizing the rest of the collection should be explored.

3   No, it should be a policy decision that whole collections only are to be digitized and that individual items within a collection should not receive higher priority simply because of present demand levels.

In an ideal world with unlimited funding, the third scenario would clearly be the recommended approach. However, in reality one constantly faces limited time and money, and competing priorities. Therefore, the third scenario, which in addition relies on the ability to define a collection (ie where it begins and ends) is often impossible to implement. It is suggested, therefore, that although the complete digitization of an archive is always the ultimate goal, it is often unattainable. Furthermore, although the second scenario retains a sense of fairness, particularly in a system of distributed collections, it could be very difficult to administrate. In reality, then, the first scenario is the one which will be most commonly adopted, but it is recommended that *wherever possible* complete digitization of an archive should be the goal.

Assessing and selecting: the matrix approach

If one is resigned to only being able to digitize part of a collection (ie high-demand items, ones in need of conservation etc), then there is a clear need to define the selection criteria that might be employed. The most preferred way to do this is to use a matrix covering all the varying categories by which an item in the archive can be assessed. It is then a matter of making sure that all representative categories are cross-checked, to give a balanced view of the collection. Pilot projects may also wish to select items which can present challenges for digitization, so that potential problems for a future more comprehensive project will be encountered early on.

An example of a similar (though less developed) matrix can be found in Ayris (1999), but its precedent lies in the earlier work by Harvard University with its *Selection for digitizing: a decision-making matrix* (available at **http://preserve. harvard.edu/resources/digitization/selection.html**) and the University of California's *Selection criteria for digitization* (available at **http://www.library. ucsb.edu/ucppp/digselec.html**). The rest of this chapter is devoted to this whole selection and assessment procedure, building on some of the ideas already established in Chapter 1, and as will become apparent the decision matrix approach has been adopted here.

Constructing the decision matrix

Dealing with the original request

We have already stated that the original request or proposal for digitization may come from a variety of sources but once it has been received one can begin to process and deal with the proposal. The first point to check is whether the digitization has been already undertaken. Many of the items held at an institution may not be unique and therefore it is possible that another project elsewhere has already converted the requested material. Similarly, it is possible that existing surrogates (such as microfilms, photographs or published facsimiles) are currently satisfying prevailing levels of demand, which may mean that one should be looking to other projects which are in more pressing need of digitization. To this end, then, the first questions in the proposed decision matrix would be:

1   Is there an existing surrogate (digital or analog) either in-house or at a remotely accessible location that covers the 'collection' proposed?
2   If there is, does the surrogate satisfy all the needs envisaged for the item?

At this point, if it is decided (probably by the appropriate subject experts) that the surrogates which already exist are good enough for any foreseeable user requests, then a project may be stopped. On the other hand, if the existing surrogates are not of sufficient standard, difficult to access or in a format unsuitable for predicted future demand (eg one can only perform very limited image analysis on a microform), then the project may continue. The appropriate decision matrix would appear as in Figure 2.1.

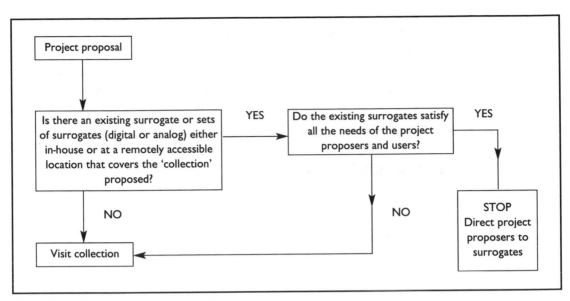

Fig. 2.1   *First steps in the project life-cycle*

Scoping the project

Once an initial surrogate check has been performed it is advised that the next decision stage is to get a basic familiarity with the item or items making up the proposed collection. There is no substitute here for actually visiting the material itself in order to get a feel for the problems that may arise. This should be conducted in collaboration with a subject expert, who will be able to answer questions related to the coverage of the material, a conservation expert, and a digitization specialist, who will be able to see any possible problems at the capturing stage (the digitization assessment discussed later). The aims at this stage are:

- to get an accurate view of the number and identity of the items that will go into the digital collection, their nature (eg medium, physical dimensions and so on) and their condition
- to identify, through the knowledge of the subject expert and appropriate users, the main reasons for digitizing, and the foreseeable demands placed upon the digital objects by the end–users (eg what is the smallest level of detail the user will need to see?)

- to receive feedback from the holder of the collection and conservation experts on what processes would be considered acceptable during the conversion process (eg can the material be scanned directly from source, can it be removed from the building, and what are the possibilities of avoiding disbinding?).

To assist in this process a sample interview sheet has been compiled and is presented in Appendix B. In practice this has proved to be extremely useful in focusing on all the issues that will need to be addressed.

Much of the material gathered at this stage will feed directly into what is known as the *digitization assessment* – ie what scanning methods are appropriate (discussed in detail in Chapter 3). However, it is safe enough for now to state that, having conducted the visit and spoken to any resident experts, one should have a reasonably accurate overview of the project itself – its scope, aims, possibilities and potential problems.

Copyright: a major hurdle

The status of the copyright on the material proposed for digitization will have major implications for the project. A fuller discussion of copyright is given in Chapter 5, but at this stage it can be stated that there are four possible situations that may arise:

1   The material is out of copyright.
2   The material is in copyright but the rights to re-use it are securable.
3   The material is in copyright but the ease by which the rights to re-use can be secured is unknown.
4   The material is in copyright and securing the rights to use it will be difficult or impossible.

How one tackles each of these will depend greatly on the resources available for negotiating copyright (in terms of both the money and the flexibility of the overall timescale). If an institution finds that it has limited means for copyright negotiation, then it may well be wise to veto immediately any projects that propose to use any material that is still in copyright or, more probably, any material that would involve prolonged negotiations for the rights. The appropriate decision matrix is given in Figure 2.2.

It is crucial to note that, after this point, the decision has been made to proceed with a more formal assessment of the project. At the moment the project is still simply a proposal that has only undergone a cursory assessment, surrogacy and copyright check. Yet it is very probable that this proposal would be one of many on the table, and there will be a need to establish some form of prioritization. To do this effectively we need to expand the discussion of the advantages and disadvantages of digitization referred to in Chapter 1. Arms (1996) noted that:

> Factors that influence selection for conversion include uniqueness of the materials, synergy with other activities in custodial divisions (such as preservation), the availability of suitable digitizing technology, and the value of the materials for education.

In an earlier study (looking at more traditional reformatting), Atkinson (1986) classified documents into 'artifactual/historical value', 'actively used items with low

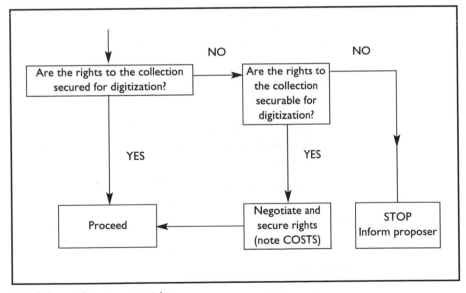

Fig. 2.2   *Covering copyright*

artifactual value' and 'little-used with low artifactual value'. Yet, however acceptable, these terms do seem to imply a distancing between the selection process and the real pressures and constraints many projects experience. For the purposes of the matrix presented here, then, three distinct areas are offered for analysis:

- increasing access
- meeting preservation needs
- matching institutional strategies.

Increasing access

In Chapter 1 it was argued that most librarians and curators consider increasing access to resources as one of the main advantages of digitization. Gould and Ebdon (1999) reinforced this assumption in their survey, with all the libraries and archives questioned stating that they selected material for digitization because of its 'historical and cultural value' and the potential to 'increase access'. Ayris (1998) also sides heavily with this policy, arguing:

> There is no point in selecting materials for digitization if there is no support for using the resource amongst target user groups. This tenet is identical to guidance in a conventional collection development policy. No paper material would be purchased by a library if potential use could not be identified amongst library users.

A digital file, properly managed and distributed, can allow users to see high-quality facsimiles more cheaply, easily and quickly. The user in question could be a researcher, a teacher wishing to locate material for class, a cataloguer, a publisher, a member of the general public and so on. A digital file can be copied without any degradation, thus vastly increasing the possibilities for dissemination; and with the Internet access becoming all-pervasive at the moment, the web offers a golden opportunity for widening the use of hitherto guarded treasures.

Even a commercial firm (when embarking on a digitization initiative) would probably share these sentiments. Simple economic theory dictates that if demand is high for an item then you increase supply. In the traditional world one is limited by the speed of the reprographics, or the availability of printed facsimiles, yet the Internet demands a remodelling of economic theory. A single item placed on the web can be accessed for an almost unlimited amount of time from anywhere in the world with no cost to the supplier. In a sense this takes all the advantages of the economic theory of *perfect competition* (unlimited supply constantly matching demand) with that of the *monopoly* (a single product and point of production).

However, simply accepting that increasing access to a resource is an advantage does not actually help much in prioritizing one collection over another. For this, instead, one needs to consider the nature (or value) of the item that is being targeted, the follow-on benefits to the user and other ancillary effects. So under the generic heading of 'increasing access' we could define the following more specific advantages:

Items in the collection are in high demand

It is common to target items that are already experiencing medium to high levels of demand for fairly obvious reasons, ie satisfying the majority of users, increased sales and so on. What is considered a high level of demand, however, will vary from institution to institution, but common ways of measuring this would be user requests, orders already placed for traditional surrogates, or existing demand for digital copies.

Items are of key historical or intellectual importance

It is certainly true that digitization tends to focus on ancient, rare and unique items (such as artefacts, manuscripts and old books), especially in libraries, museums and galleries. However, one may also occasionally target more recent material (such as 20th-century journals or newspapers). These items may not necessarily be in high demand at the moment but could benefit from *wider knowledge about their existence*. Conversion and appropriate dissemination could also allow these items to be accessible more easily both *within* the institution (eg on an intranet) and *remotely*.

Items in the collection have been withdrawn from circulation

In some instances, the items may be so valuable or in such a fragile state that they have been withdrawn from public access altogether and placed in conservation. A digital copy of the item will reintroduce it to the public without any security risk or the danger of possibly further damaging the original.

Items will form part of a collaborative venture

It has been noted already that digitization projects are widespread and are being undertaken in almost all areas of society. Therefore it is possible that the collection proposed at your institution may *supplement* one already available. Similarly, collaborative projects can allow collections to be *virtually reassembled*. It may be that over time sections of collections have been sold off or dispersed around the globe; these can now be brought together again in a virtual space.

Functionality will be increased

A digital file can be copied continually without any notable degradation. Similarly the electronic copy can be subjected to all kinds of image-processing techniques, again without harming the original or the digital master. Users will be able to select sections, move them to other documents for comparison or into other applications for further analysis. Furthermore, assuming that the digital items are catalogued to a minimum standard (ie there is *sufficient metadata* – a term explained in Chapter 5), then the user will be able to navigate the collection more easily locating items in a shorter space of time (and thus increasing the chances of them coming across new areas of interest).

Drawing all the above together in terms of increasing access, we could define a complete check-list of the demands that would be met by digitizing a collection as shown in Figure 2.3.

Meeting preservation needs

The notion of digitizing for preservation is one that is often central to many

---

Increase access
What demands will be met, in terms of increasing access, if the collection is digitized?

❏ Items in collection are in high demand.

❏ Project would reinstate material into circulation that up to now has been withdrawn (eg for conservation or security reasons).

❏ Project would make items of key historical or intellectual content more widely accessible within the host institution.

❏ Project would make items of key historical or intellectual content more widely accessible outside the host institution.

❏ Project would increase demand for, or interest in, items in the collection which up to now have been relatively ignored.

❏ Assuming appropriate metadata and access facilities, the project would make the collection easier to navigate and would allow the user to locate desired items more quickly.

❏ Digital surrogates would add functionality to the way the collection is used (eg allow for image analysis of damaged material).

❏ Project will increase availability of material with direct relevance to teaching.

❏ Project will supplement existing accessible digital collections (held locally or remotely).

❏ Project will virtually reassemble a collection.

❏ Project will satisfy existing requests for digital surrogates from users

---

Fig.2.3   *Increasing access by digitization*

initiatives. In Chapter 1 it was suggested that in effect the jury is still out over whether one can rely on the digital object as an archival format. It has been suggested, on the one hand, that it is indeed possible to define a standard quality for digital objects that satisfies archival requirements. This would meet preservation needs, acting as an alternative for other forms of surrogate (eg a printed facsimile on non-acid-based paper, microfilm or microfiche). In theory, then, the digital object would retain all significant information contained in the original document(s) and, under appropriately stringent conditions, should survive forever.

Needless to say, the attractions of such a proposal are obvious. Some collections are in dire need of preservation or migrating to a more robust format. As Frey and Reilly (1999, 1) note:

The materials that make up photographs . . . are not chemically stable. Environmental issues such as light, chemical agents, heat, humidity, and storage conditions affect and destroy photographic material. In a general way, the life span of photographs can be extended only by appropriate storage . . . [yet they] are facing a dilemma: on one hand, photographic documents must be stored under correct climatic conditions, and, on the other hand, it is often necessary to have quick access to them.

However, there is still considerable unease at the prospect of relying on any digital copy as a substitute for other preservation formats. As Arms (1996) notes:

One issue that cannot be adequately addressed here is an ongoing topic of discussion at the Library: the potential for digital versions to serve as preservation copies. Traditionally, preservation of content has focussed on creating a facsimile, as faithful a copy of the original as feasible, on a long-lasting medium. The most widely accepted method for preserving the information in textual materials is microfilming and for pictorial materials is photographic reproduction.

The particular problem with digital files is the preservation of the digital data, and the life-cycle management of digital data, stemming often from a lack of a long-term institutional commitment to its maintenance. It is very rare to find any institution that has a fully comprehensive policy in place to guarantee the active migration and refreshment of digital objects to ensure longevity of access (a point that will be elaborated upon in Chapter 5). Many of the variables involved in such a process are as yet unknown, and where they are known it is clear such maintenance involves considerable cost for the host archive. It is for this reason that in the UK CURL (Consortium of University Research Libraries) launched the CEDARS (CURL Exemplars for Digital Archives) project (available at **http://www.leeds.ac.uk/cedars/**), noting that:

Recent years have seen a massive increase in the range and volume of digital information resources, and their acquisition by libraries, but there is no formal mechanism for the long-term preservation of this material. There is a pressing need for a strategy for digital preservation.

The CEDARS project itself builds on the seminal US report produced in 1996 by the Research Libraries Group and Commission on Preservation and Access (*Preserving digital information*, available at **http://www.rlg.ac.uk/ArchTF/** or **http://www.rlg.org/ArchTF/**).

Chapman, Conway, and Kenney (1999) have conducted the most recent study of these issues. Comparing the digitization activities at Cornell and Yale Universities, the study focuses on 'The future of the hybrid approach for the preservation of brittle books'. It notes that 'despite predictions that microfilm could be replaced by digital imaging, many have come to appreciate that digitization may increase access to materials but it does not guarantee their continued preservation.' The study rests on the assumption that 'until digital preservation capabilities can be broadly implemented and shown to be cost-effective, microfilm remains the primary reformatting strategy' with reformating being the only viable strategy for the preservation of brittle paper, and that 'although digital imaging can be used to enhance access, preservation goals will not be considered met until a microfilm copy or computer output microfilm recording of digital image files has been produced that satisfies national standards for quality and permanence.'

Where digitization can help in preservation is, of course, in the deflection of demand to view the original document. Most holders of rare or valuable material are acutely aware of the damage that repeated handling can do to the original document, and are constantly seeking to limit this access. In some cases, where the document is in a particularly bad state of repair (or is classed as being a security risk), the material may have to be withdrawn from general use, and might only be made available to satisfy the most pressing of research needs, or not at all in some cases. The availability of a high-resolution digital surrogate can then be of help to the curator, as it will act as another possibility for the researcher instead of handling the original. As Noerr (1998) notes:

> Physical handling is one of the most destructive things that can happen to a fragile object. One of the best ways to preserve it is to limit physical access to it. This is a very strong case for creating a digital library.

Meeting preservation needs
What demands will be met, in terms of preservation, if the collection is digitized?

❏ The project will fulfil the needs of preservation, for the original item(s), either via the digital surrogate or by outputting to an accepted analog preservation medium.

❏ The project will fulfil the needs of 'rescue digitization' by reducing damage (eg via handling) of the original.

Fig. 2.4   *Preservation issues*

Yet this should not detract from the unavoidable truth that any copy, be it digital or microform, can only serve as a surrogate, not as a complete replacement for the original. Even with microfilm no surrogate has ever been regarded as a perpetual preservation copy of the original item and this rule should equally be applied to digitization. Above all, there should be no detraction from the continued efforts to preserve the original.

Returning to the decision matrix, then, we can now add further criteria to help us select and prioritize collections and projects proposed for digitization. In terms of matching preservation needs we can reduce our questions down to the two choices shown in Figure 2.4.

Matching institutional strategies

The opening section of this book, with its declaration by the British Prime Minister Tony Blair, clearly illustrates the political baggage that surrounds digitization. Recognition of institutional and commercial strategies at both national and local level is extremely important if the project is to succeed and prosper. The decision matrix therefore has to include a list of categories indicating whether the collection adheres to these policies. Under the generic heading of 'matching institutional strategies', one could define the following more specific advantages:

Reducing costs and burden on existing resources

The availability of a digital facsimile of an object may lead to a decrease in the pressure on already overstretched resources. For example, a digitization project that made available texts on a reading list for a large body of students could well lead to a decrease in photocopying requests.

Generating income

It has been already established that one of the main advantages of digital objects is that they can be easily accessed. Extending the argument, one could also state that digital objects can be easily distributed, or sold, possibly through a developed e-commerce system, generating income for more conversion projects. It should also be recognized that an online presence *raises the profile of an institution or company*, especially if it is making available items of high value. This in turn may have a snowball effect, *attracting more income from external sources* (such as by increasing the chances in grant applications, or drawing potential sponsors to the institution).

Increasing awareness

As well as raising the profile of an institution, the digital project may increase knowledge of a particular collection, subject or product. More importantly, from a strategic perspective, initiating a digitization project in an area which has been previously sidelined in other initiatives can send a strong message about institutional commitment to that discipline.

Institutional support

In a devolved environment, such as a dispersed library system or an educational establishment, it is essential that the digitization project can demonstrate clear local support (from the librarian or curator in charge of the items, or from academics who may use it in their teaching) as well as following the institution's IT strategy.

Ancillary effects

In addition to the more obvious advantages listed above, there are several ancillary pluses that may impact upon the host institution. First, the project itself could well lead to a *raising of the skills level* of the staff involved. A localizing of talent and expertise will be of advantage to other initiatives. Alternatively, it is highly likely that it will increase the hardware and software base at your institution that can be drawn on by other projects.

To complete the decision matrix, then, one would need to add an expanded checklist relating to institutional strategies (see Figure 2.5).

Meeting institutional strategies
What demands will be met, in terms of institutional strategies, if the collection is digitized?

❑ Project will reduce costs or burden on staff (eg retrieving documents, arranging surrogates).

❑ Project has potential to generate income through marketing.

❑ Project has potential to attract funding.

❑ Project has potential to attract or promote digital capture of supplementary material/analogous material.

❑ Collection is based in a subject area which has been neglected in previous digitization initiatives.

❑ Collection is drawn (mainly) from a department or section that has had little involvement in previous digitization initiatives.

❑ Project will raise the skills level of staff.

❑ Project has aesthetic appeal.

❑ Project has support from all appropriate parties.

Fig. 2.5   *Meeting institutional strategies*

Putting all of this together, we are presented with the matrix shown in Figure 2.6.

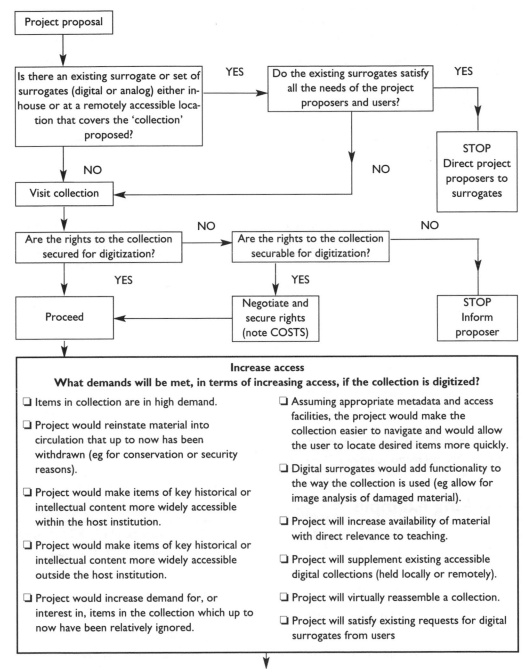

Fig. 2.6   *The full matrix* (continued overleaf)

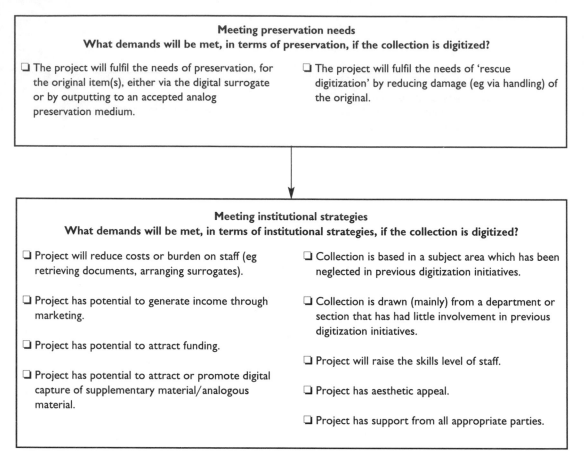

Meeting preservation needs
What demands will be met, in terms of preservation, if the collection is digitized?

❑ The project will fulfil the needs of preservation, for the original item(s), either via the digital surrogate or by outputting to an accepted analog preservation medium.

❑ The project will fulfil the needs of 'rescue digitization' by reducing damage (eg via handling) of the original.

Meeting institutional strategies
What demands will be met, in terms of institutional strategies, if the collection is digitized?

❑ Project will reduce costs or burden on staff (eg retrieving documents, arranging surrogates).

❑ Project has potential to generate income through marketing.

❑ Project has potential to attract funding.

❑ Project has potential to attract or promote digital capture of supplementary material/analogous material.

❑ Collection is based in a subject area which has been neglected in previous digitization initiatives.

❑ Collection is drawn (mainly) from a department or section that has had little involvement in previous digitization initiatives.

❑ Project will raise the skills level of staff.

❑ Project has aesthetic appeal.

❑ Project has support from all appropriate parties.

Fig. 2.6   *The full matrix* (continued from previous page)

A working example

In order to understand how such a decision matrix may be employed in the working environment, let us take a hypothetical example through the decision trees to explore where the matrix takes us.

Most collections proposed for digitization tend to stem from an awareness of their rare value. Therefore, the hypothetical example used below concentrates on a collection of books owned (but not written) by Charles Dickens, which contain numerous annotations by the author and are thus of extreme interest to Dickens scholars. The books all date from the early part of the 19th century (and hence are out of copyright) and were sold as a single collection to a national museum in the early 1920s. The museum is keen to establish itself as a national centre of excellence in IT and sees digitization as a way of doing this. It has begun a survey of all of its collections to see which ones should be prioritized for conversion, in the knowledge that national funding is soon to be made available for such projects.

The initial surrogate check yields the following information. So far the collection itself has not been digitized, locally or remotely, though it is clearly in high demand. Some microfilm surrogates are available (but they were made in the 1950s and are of questionable quality). However, no printed facsimiles exist of any of the material. In summary, then, it could be stated that at present the surrogates that exist (ie the film) are sporadic in their coverage and do not satisfy all the demands of the users on account of their rarity (limited access) and the poor quality of the microfilms. Thus digitization does seem to hold some advantages.

The next stage according to the matrix would be to visit the collection and interview the curator in charge in order to get an accurate view of the number and nature of the items involved (using the interview sheet in Appendix B). It is soon discovered that the collection only numbers 50 titles, all of which are printed bound volumes of around A5 in size, and in extremely good condition. The binding is not so tight that it prohibits opening the book. Of the 50 volumes, ten are notable as they contain numerous annotations by Dickens in his own hand and are in extremely high demand, but even so the whole collection is regarded as noteworthy. The curator feels that the collection would benefit from digitization, even though the collection is widely known about already, as it would reduce demand for the originals. However, security concerns create considerable reluctance with regard to any suggestion to remove the collection to an external location for digitization (or out-sourcing, as explained in Chapter 4). Overall the curator did not feel that the digitization process would present any problems regarding the conservation of the material and was happy for the project to proceed.

With this information in mind it is worth looking at the collection in terms of the categories listed in the matrix. With reference to increasing access, the collection is clearly in high demand (as is most unique material related to

Dickens) and of key historical value. It is debatable whether digitization would increase knowledge of the collection itself as most scholars are already aware of its existence, but if the policy of free Internet access were adopted it would clearly be of benefit to scholars both within and outside the host country. The items have not been withdrawn from public access as such, though this may happen in the future. However, thanks to the enormous interest in the works of Dickens and the proliferation of material related to him, it is clear that this could easily be part of a larger collaborative project with other institutions (eg publishers, libraries or universities). The project plan is to simply present digital images of the pages in question with sufficient catalogue information (ie not to fully transcribe all the annotations), so functionality would not be increased greatly beyond assisting browsing and searching at a catalogue entry level.

The interview revealed that the material itself is in good condition and is not deteriorating of its own accord. Therefore preservation issues are not central to the reasons behind digitization, but the librarian has welcomed any reduction in the handling of the originals (ie rescue digitization). The project, though, will fulfil many of the current strategies of the museum: it will raise its profile globally, it will raise the skills level of the staff involved, and has the full support of the senior managers and curators involved. Although there will not be any noticeable reduction in the existing burden on staff, and money is being received from a national grant body so that the scope for generating income is often limited, it is hoped that this project would be a good flagship to launch the museum's digitization initiative and help to attract money in the future to tackle its other collections. Finishing the step-by-step progress through the matrix, then, it is clear that the collection scores highly in the 'increasing access' section and moderately well under 'preservation' and 'institutional strategies'.

Using the decision matrix in the real world

The presentation of the decision matrix and flowchart above, seems to imply a rather systematic approach to assessment, which is both comforting and dangerous. It is always reassuring to be presented with a series of check-boxes that one simply ticks or crosses in answer to a series of questions demanding a yes or no answer (or in this case a prioritization). Yet this is misleading. The above questions are guidelines and are of a generic kind. Some of them may be irrelevant to your company or institution while at the same time there may be significant omissions (notably from the perspective of anyone working in the purely commercial market). Similarly, the systematic approach will not be appropriate in some cases. Not only is it a time-consuming activity to perform this on a large number of collections, but it may be inappropriate if it seems glaringly obvious which collections one would prioritize.

Similarly, one should note that there is no weighting attached to any of the categories or questions contained under them. Nor is it suggested that to rank collections one could simply add up the number of ticks under each section. Both systems would be impractical as different sets of circumstances and institutions would demand different weightings. For example, a public library or publishing house would probably rank several of the sections under 'increasing access' much higher than a copyright or legal deposit library (which is more concerned with the preservation of the item).

It is suggested, however, that an initial survey of all collections using the above matrix would be of use in most institutions, as it would help to prepare for unplanned funding opportunities. Once one has established a clear picture of all the collections that could possibly be offered for conversion, it is a simple exercise to assess all of them using the matrix, possibly throwing up some interesting results. Most importantly, it would demonstrate to any funding body that the assessment and evaluation of collections was taken seriously and that a considered analysis had already been undertaken. At the very least, following the completion of such an exercise, all the collections could be now ranked in terms of low, medium or high under each of the three categories. This would allow for a quick response to any future calls for projects. As an added bonus it would also produce a detailed document of all collections, and this would be an attractive document to circulate amongst potential sponsors or benefactors.

Chapter summary

This chapter has covered:

- why one needs to assess collections prior to digitizing them
- how a digitization project can fulfil the goals of increasing access to collections, preserving original documents and meeting institutional strategies
- a working matrix to allow for the assessment and prioritization of collections.

3 | How do you digitize?

Introduction

Digitization is at the core of the digital project. Although this may seem an obvious statement to make, it is worth repeating as many project managers are tempted to dismiss the conversion stage as a simple process – when clearly it is anything but. To get to grips with this stage, however, and the rest of the initial stages of a project (the digitization assessment), one needs to be comfortable with how the digitization process actually works – not only the technical issues of the digital image, but also such problems as hardware, software and resulting file formats. This chapter sets out a series of explanations that cover the basic technical information needed to understand the processes behind digitization. In no way should these be seen as comprehensive in their coverage, and the further reading section at the end of the book points to other publications which will provide more detailed technical guidelines. Readers who are mainly concerned with the management of digital imaging projects may wish to leave this topic for the time being, and move directly to the section on digitization assessment, where the workflow idea will be picked up again. However, it is strongly recommended that everyone involved in a digital imaging project should take the time to familiarize themselves at some point with the core issues discussed below.

A definition: scanning or digitization?

Throughout this book the words scanning and digitization are used synonymously, in keeping with standard practice. However, purists will state that there are distinct differences between the two. Scanning involves the conversion of specifically *image*-based analog material into digital form. Digitization, on the other hand, means the conversion of *any* analog material into electronic storage, including sound and video. In other words, all scanning is digitization, but not all digitization is scanning. For the purposes of this book, however, which focuses purely on the digital image, both words effectively mean the same.

For ease of definition, then, scanning and digitization imply the conversion of analog images into digital images. To perform this you will need the following:

- the source item
- a capture device, such as a scanner or digital camera
- a computer complete with the necessary software to interface with the scanner
- computer storage to house the digital image.

Understanding digital imaging

To proceed with imaging, one needs to get a clear picture of what exactly is involved in digital imaging. In order to do this, there are three important areas which need to be addressed:

- the anatomy of the digital image
- digital image file formats
- digitization hardware and software.

Once these have been addressed, one can then look at the way digitization fits into the life-cycle of the project, first in the digitization assessment and then in the actual workflow of conversion.

The anatomy of a digital image: dots, pixels, and resolutions

The standard desktop computer consists of a central processing unit (CPU), a monitor, and peripherals such as a keyboard, a mouse, spare hard-drives and so on. Those interested in digital imaging should begin by concerning themselves with the monitor. A close examination of any computer screen will reveal that it is made up of a series of small 'cells', each one displaying black, white, grey or a colour. The machine being used to write this book, for example, is currently set so that at the moment there are 1024 of these cells running horizontally across the screen and 768 vertically. In computer jargon the screen is set to a resolution of 1024 × 768 (and one could choose from 640 × 480 up to 1600 × 1200).

The screen resolution need not concern us for now. Instead we are interested in what actually goes into these cells, or dots, or to use the correct term *picture elements*, usually abbreviated to *pixels* – all 786,432 of them on the screen at the moment. The simple answer would be to say that each pixel is filled by black, white, a shade of grey or a colour: it can never have nothing in it unless it is broken! The question then remains: how does the computer know which colour or shade it should fill each pixel with? For our purposes, this should be phrased as: how does the computer know how to reassemble a digital image on the screen with each pixel resembling the original colour of the document?

The process behind all of this is not too difficult to understand, but at the same time has extremely important implications for how one digitizes an item. Each colour and shade of colour (or black, white, grey) is given a unique code by the computer. Like all computer information these unique codes are each stored as a binary code – a series of ones or zeros. At the simplest level this would be a one-figure code – eg '0' equals black and '1' equals white. Therefore, if the computer was told that a certain pixel had the code '0' associated with it, it would fill that individual pixel with black, and so on. According to this scenario we would describe the image as a *one-bit image* (only a single bit is needed for each pixel – ie a '1' or a '0'). Each pixel would be described as having a depth of two (ie there are two possible values it can be filled with or associated to – again '1' or '0').

If we were to imagine, therefore, a black-and-white image that covered the whole screen at 1024 × 768 pixels, it would be made up of 786,432 pixels, each with a value of '1' or '0' attached to them displaying either black or white. The codes for these pixels are stored and processed in the computer's memory as a grid or map of bits (hence *bitmap*). When instructed (eg by a piece of software), the computer will convert these codes to the appropriate colour (in this case black or white) and project them onto the display screen so that from a distance

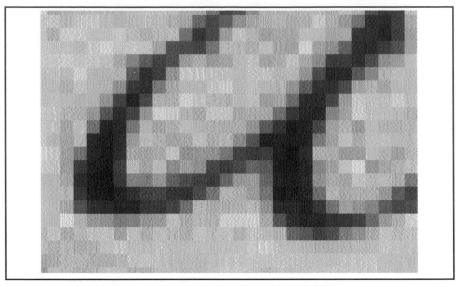

Fig. 3.1   *Jagged edges*

it looks like a normal image. This process is actually performed by an electronic beam that traces back and forth horizontally from left to right, and vertically from top to bottom, filling in each pixel.

This type of image is termed a *raster graphic* – it is storing the image as a series of independent dots. If one zooms in or enlarges a raster graphic too much, jagged edges, or blocking, will be visible, as can be seen in Figure 3.1.

Yet it is clear that each pixel can hold much more information than just black or white. Every day on our screens we see shades of grey and colour – but what exactly are we seeing? The important word here is *shade*, indicating that there is the possibility of increasing the number of variants in the image (we are not just limited to black or white). The next question then is how do we control and measure the number of different shades we are actually seeing? The answer will depend on the image itself, namely how much depth can be applied to it. In the above example it was a one-bit image, but if we were to say an image was *four-bit*, we would say it would have four slots or codes it could fill, again with ones or zeros. The one-bit image could have a value of either 1 or 0, whereas the four-bit image could have as many as 16 values:

0000	1010
0001	0101
0010	0111
0100	1110
1000	1111
0011	1001
0110	1011
1100	1101

In other words there are 16 possible values for each cell. We call this a four-bit image because four binary digits are used to represent each pixel – hence the term *bit-depth*. Therefore, if this was a greyscale image, then each cell could be filled by any one of 16 possible shades of grey (with '0000' being black, and '1111' being white). Without repeating this exercise, it can be stated that an eight-bit image would imply 256 different combinations, ie 2^8 ('00000000', '11111111' and every possible pattern of eight made up of zeros and ones in between). A 16-bit image, therefore, would have 2^{16} or 65,536 possible patterns, and a 24-bit graphic would have 16,777,216 or over 16 million different combinations. In the real world, this means that if we were digitizing an image as a greyscale at eight bits, each cell or pixel could contain one of 256 shades of grey. Similarly, if we were digitizing in colour at 24 bits, each pixel could be filled with one of over 16 million colours. It is this fine control of gradation from cell to cell that produces the high-quality images we see in many digital imaging projects.

Clearly, then, varying the bit-depth allows one much greater control over what each cell or pixel on the screen will contain. However, the other ingredient in the formula of how good the image will look is termed *resolution*. This relates to the number of pixels used to convey the image itself and is determined when one digitizes the source item. The resolution is expressed as 'dpi', which stands for dots per inch, with the inch referring to an inch of the original item.

For example, let us consider scanning in an image that is 10 inches long by 5 inches wide. The scanner or digital camera could be set to digitize at 100 dots per inch (100 dpi), which would mean that each square inch of the original item would be captured at a resolution of 100 pixels by 100 pixels. Multiplying the dpi by the size of the original item, we would say that the digital image would measure 1000 pixels (on the long side) by 500 pixels – ie we now have a record of the pixel dimensions. The rule of thumb would be that the more dots per inch you digitize at, the higher the quality of the image – or to put it more simply, you are recording more information about each square inch of the original item.

There is one major problem, however, that often arises with resolution. This concerns the size of the image scanned compared with the original dimensions of the object. To understand this, let us assume we have a surrogate – in this case a microfilm – of an original item. Let us state that we capture the microfilm at 8500 dpi. At first this may sound like an exceedingly high resolution. However, this does not take into account the size of the original item and the reduction ratio used in capturing to film. For example, if the microfilm was one inch square, but the original item measured ten inches square the reduction ratio (RR) is 10:1 – it has been reduced to a tenth of its original size. This needs to be applied to the capture resolution of 8500 bringing it down to an *effective* dpi of 850 (this example was taken from Robinson (1993, 16). A figure of 850 dpi would still seem high to most people involved in digitization, but the important point to note is that the resolution at which one chooses to scan is not always the 'effective' resolution one ends up with if the physical dimensions of the original object are taken into account.

If, however, the original item had measured 20 inches square we would say the reduction ratio would be 20. Using the simple formula of:

Effective dpi = dpi setting of the capture device/reduction ratio

One would say that in this scenario the *effective* dpi is reduced to 425:

8500/20 = 425

Robinson also noted other features which may reduce the effective dpi of 850 even lower – such as the blurred boundaries between contrasts on the original item with those of the computer pixel (known as the Nyquist sample error (Robinson, 1993, 20). However, recent developments, such as Microsoft's ClearType may well help to remedy such problems in the near future (this is currently available for the displaying of images, but should also be available for the capturing of material).

This is the type of issue one would need to bear in mind when looking at buying a camera. Although the hardware specification may boast proudly of an impressive pixel array (ie the number of pixels it can capture along the vertical and horizontal axes) one would need to examine this in terms of the original document to consider what the effective dpi will be. The above formula is fairly standard but in this instance it has been taken from Kenney and Chapman (1996b). In their extensive study of the mechanics of digitization they explore in depth the problems that might arise from the above, and manufacturers' claims that need to be checked concerning digitization equipment. For the purposes of this book, which is looking at the wider context of the digitization process, the reader need only be alerted to the possibilities of such problems but should be aware of them nevertheless.

It is at this point that one should briefly mention the concepts of *threshold* and *dynamic range*. Threshold is the simplest to define as it merely refers to a setting for digitizing bi-tonal images at which grey pixels will be interpreted as black or white (in effect this appears to most people as changing the contrast). The threshold values usually range from 0 to 255. Threshold is particularly important if the documents being scanned are textual and are to be subsequently processed by optical character recognition (OCR) software (see Chapter 5). Dynamic range is a record of how much density there is in the image, which is calculated by taking brightness readings between absolute white and absolute black. In other words, it reflects the changes in tone, and when the term is applied to digitization equipment it implies the difference between the lightest tones and the darkest tones that they can detect. The density (D) is scaled on a rating of 0 to 4, and scanners will often state their minimum rating (Dmin) as something like 0.2, and their maximum (Dmax) as a figure like 3.2. In this case the dynamic range would be 3.0 (ie the difference between the Dmin and the Dmax). The greater the dynamic range, the greater the image detail in dark shadow areas of the image. A scanner which offers 24-bit capture may offer a dynamic range of 2.5, whereas a 30-bit scanner may push it up to 3.0, thus recording more detail in the darker areas. In summary, although bit-depth and dpi are probably the most important factors that will influence image quality, there are also others such as dynamic range. These factors are sometimes dictated by the hardware one has to use – an issue we shall return to again later on.

To this discussion we should also add some brief remarks on *colour space*. This is sometimes known as the *colour model* or *gamut*, and refers to the spectra used to represent colours in an image. The most common ones encountered are RGB (red, green, blue), used in monitors, and CMYK (cyan, magenta, yellow, black), used mainly in printing. The most common manifestation of these will be when image files are printed out. The paper copy may yield different colours from the ones on the screen (though there are considerable efforts being made to address this problem, notably through the International Colour Consortium). However, overall this will not cause undue concern for most projects.

Digitization quality: the trade-off

Given what we have covered so far, it is natural enough to ask why one does not always digitize at the highest level possible. Bearing in mind that 24-bit capture provides a very high range of colours, for example, and that the higher the dpi the better the image, surely it is in everyone's interest simply to go for the maximum quality. Well, yes and no. In a perfect world one would probably always adopt this line of approach; yet digital projects are undertaken in the real world with financial pressures and time constraints.

The most frequently cited reason for not choosing the maximum resolution is the resulting file size. Although computer storage is now much cheaper than it was, high-resolution images still mean large files, which in turn cost money to store. This can be of particular concern if one has to move the images around networks for delivery or post-processing. Thankfully, there is a standard formula for calculating file size which is reasonably straightforward:

Resulting file size = (dpi × dpi × bit-depth × dimensions of original item in inches (height × width))/8

This will present one with the file size in bytes (hence the division by eight). Let us consider a simple example of a 1-inch square item being scanned at 100 dpi, at 1 bit (which means either black or white). Using our formula this would imply:

Resulting file size = 100 × 100 × 1 × 1 (1 × 1) = 10,000/8 = 1250 bytes or 1.25 Kb

At the other extreme let us consider a 10 inch square item being scanned in 24-bit colour at a resolution of 600 dpi. This time the formula would be:

Resulting file size = 600 × 600 × 24 × 100 (10 × 10) = 864,000,000/8 = 108,000,000 bytes or 108, 000 Kb or 108 Mb

Clearly, in this latter case, the file size is extremely large – equivalent to over 75 floppy disks – and nine such images would nearly fill a 1-Gb hard drive. For an informative study of the range of file sizes a single image can create it is recommended one looks at Tanner and Lomax's paper *Future technologies for preserving the past* (Tanner and Lomax, 1999b). In this paper the authors compare a range of formats and cross-reference them with varying resolutions and bit-depths to show the possible resulting file sizes (1 Mb up to 440 Mb).

There are other reasons, however, why one may not wish to digitize at the highest possible quality. Firstly, high-resolution digital cameras can often take several minutes to capture each image, and the throughput may be as low as 15 images an hour. If one is looking to run a service that provides a speedy turnaround, then one may have to compromise quality for speed. Most importantly, however, is the notion of digitizing material that is fit for the purpose. If the image being converted will only ever be used on the web, or is to be printed out and then discarded, or is simply of such low quality in the first place (eg a faxed document), then it may be decided that there is no point in digitizing to something as high as 24 bits.

Compression and interpolation

One solution to the balancing act of quality versus size is to employ some form of image compression. This will allow one to take the data from a file and use an encoding (and decoding) algorithm to make it much smaller. Ideally this would mean no loss of information so that the resulting file – in this case the compressed digital image – is a true representation of the original. However, many file formats (described below) provide 'lossy' (as opposed to 'lossless') compressions – which, although not necessarily obvious to the human eye, do involve a degradation in quality. Although compression techniques (the common ones being JPEG, wavelet and fractal) attempt to remove 'redundant' information about the image, they are generally not used in digital imaging projects for the master image (ie the one that is archived for future use), but are perfectly adequate for distribution purposes such as via the web. TIFF Group IV compression is an exception here and it is generally accepted that, being 'lossless', it can be used for master images of bi-tonal documents (see below for more information).

Interpolation is a phrase often used in connection with compression, but used erroneously in most instances. Interpolation actually involves 'guessing' (as opposed to compressing) by the computer when it comes to the image. As you may recall from our initial discussion, each digital image is made up of a series of pixels, and related to each pixel is a computer code that dictates how it will be filled in terms of colour and tone. However, what happens if we did not originally capture all the information we need, or we have resized the image, thus requiring the computer to 'fill in the gaps'? In both cases interpolation would be involved. A more formal definition of this is that interpolation is a way of estimating a value of a given pixel, based on knowledge about the surrounding pixels. A crude example of this would be if a pixel was flanked by pure black on one side and pure white on the other. In this case interpolation could fill the middle pixel with grey. The problem with interpolation, therefore, is that it is not a true representation of the image, as new material is being added which at best could be described as inserting missing values. Therefore, if we are interested in digitizing at a quality that is as true to the original as possible, it is best to avoid any interpolation at the capturing or resizing stage.

Digital image file formats

Now that we have discussed the basics of the digital image, it is time to move to the second category needed to get to grips with digital imaging – namely the resulting files that can be created. As with so many issues surrounding digitization, the question of choosing which file format to use to both store and deliver the images is a somewhat vexed one. From the earliest days of the operating-system wars between Apple, Microsoft, and UNIX, there have been a stream of different file formats for graphic files. Understandably this has presented considerable difficulties in the long-term usability of the files and their cross-platform delivery. Some file formats have disappeared altogether, or are only ever seen in specialized instances, whilst others are beginning to emerge as something approaching an accepted standard. When planning for digitization, project managers will be faced with two standard questions:

1   What image format should they choose as the capture standard (often used for archiving the files thereafter)?
2   What image format should they choose for the delivery to the end-user (eg when circulating the files on CD-ROM or via the web)?

Both of these questions will be directly influenced by the overall aim of the project and the user needs that it hopes to satisfy. However, in order to answer these questions, one has to survey the range of digital image file formats available.

TIFF (.TIF)

TIFF (Tagged Image File Format) is perhaps the most important image format available at the moment. It is widely used as the cross-platform and archiving format in most digitization projects, particularly as it allows for high-quality images (up to 24-bit colour) to be saved without any loss in the original capture. Furthermore it is not tied to any particular scanner or display. Conversion from TIFF to other formats is relatively straightforward and most imaging software will allow for this. Subsequently, it is becoming standard practice to create master images at a high quality in the TIFF format, save and archive them, and create derivatives from the TIFF file for subsequent delivery. TIFF offers a dual-platform choice but it is generally recommended that when saving (especially master images) you use the Intel byte order (or 'PC version') with no compression. TIFF images can be saved using the LZW method (Lempel-Ziv-Welch) of compression though, which is usually regarded as lossless, but even so most projects would not employ this when creating master images. A common term used in relation to TIFFs is *Group 4* (or *IV*) *compression*. This is in fact (Comité Consultatif International Téléphonique et Télégraphique), now known as the International Telecommunication Union) for fax documents. As it was meant to deal with the transmission of a fax, which is a black-and-white image, this protocol is also used for compressing any bi-tonal document (up to a resolution of 400 dpi). The compression ratio is usually around 25:1. Therefore digital imaging projects that are interested in scanning black-and-white images often feel safe in creating master files under Group 4 compression.

JPEG (.JPG) and GIF (.GIF)

The JPEG (Joint Photographic Experts Group) format, and the GIF (Graphical Interchange Format) are the most popular image files delivered via the web and are ideally suited for displaying in all browsers. Following on from the above discussion, many digitization projects create JPEG or GIF files from their TIFF masters for subsequent delivery via the web.

To begin with, JPEGs (more correctly JPEG File Interchange Format) are traditionally used for the display of colour images. They support 24-bit colour depth, but allow for compression (thus making the file size smaller) though this does reduce the quality. When using JPEGs for web delivery one detects a relatively slower display speed than when using GIFs, for example. This is due to the fact that JPEGs employ a dual compression and decompression algorithm. So-called progressive JPEGs allow for a speedier display as they load in a low-quality image first and gradually build up the blocks of the graphic increasing its clarity and quality.

GIF format images are also widely used on websites but mainly for line art or greyscales. This is chiefly due to the fact that GIFs only allow for 8-bit images (ie 256 values). Two versions of the GIF format are available, unhelpfully termed 87a and 89a (the latter being the more recent). Both can use a feature known as interlacing which, like with progressive JPEGs, allows one to display a low-resolution image first and then gradually fill in more detail (the benefit here is to the user, who can stop the transmission at an early stage if the image is not the one he or she wished to see). GIF images are compressed using the lossless LZW (Lempel-Ziv-Welch) method, which is also available under the TIFF format.

Photo CD (.PCD)

Kodak's Photo CD is designed to allow slides or negatives to be scanned onto CDs at a local film-developing agency. One simply takes the images in, pays the initial cost of the CD and a fee per image, and then receives the CD back containing the images. The files can be displayed on a computer monitor via a standard CD-ROM drive, but delivery over the web is not as straightforward as using JPEGs or GIFs, requiring the launching of an external viewer. Although the convenience factor does make Photo CD an attractive process, as does the range of file sizes automatically created for each image (varying from low to very high quality), many digitization projects steer away from its use, especially for archival purposes. This is chiefly because the Photo CD format uses ImagePac files – a proprietary format – as opposed to the freely available TIFF standard.

PNG (.PNG)

PNG (Portable Network Graphics) is being promoted as an alternative to the GIF format as it has some added features. As with GIF it is lossless, and can be viewed by common web browsers, but it also offers better control over image brightness, allowing up to 48 bits per pixel (as opposed to GIF's 8-bit limitation) and increased levels of transparency. As yet, however, the take-up of PNG has not been overwhelming and it remains to be seen how far this format will go.

Pyramid file formats

As discussed earlier, the problem with low-resolution images is that they are perfectly adequate for displaying on the web, but are poor for printing or for more detailed image analysis. On the other hand, high-quality images, which would allow the user to explore the graphic in much greater detail, are usually too large to be distributed across networks without problems. This has been a long-standing problem with digital imaging.

A possible solution may be available in the form of *pyramid file formats*. These are so termed because they allow you to store a range of resolutions of a particular image in the same file. At the base of the pyramid you could have the low-resolution image that can be presented initially (and quickly) to the web user as a GIF or JPEG. If users then wish to explore a section of the image in greater detail, then they can go to the next layer of the pyramid (at a higher resolution). More importantly, as the image can be broken into 'tiles' or sections, then they only need to load that piece of the image they are interested in and then bring in other sections or tiles as they see fit.

Several examples of this format are currently available. One of the most popular is the FlashPix format (.FPX) developed by Kodak, Hewlett-Packard Company, Live Picture Inc, and Microsoft, but others include GridPrix, JTIP (JPEG Tiled Image Pyramid) and MrSID (actually a highly developed use of wavelet compression). At the time of writing, the new format from the Joint Photographic Experts Group, JPEG 2000, also offers a tiled approach to compression. As with all these options, however, and especially if a wavelet compression is used, end-users may be required to download a special plug-in for their web browsers, and this may not be ideal for seamless delivery. A similar problem comes with Java Applets, which automatically download onto machines. Again, although these may offer increased image analysis, the installation (especially with public machines such as are found in reading rooms) can often be a problem.

Other formats: PICT (.PIC), BMP (.BMP), PDF (.PDF) and DjVU

Other formats abound in the imaging arena and one will often encounter a range of different formats. Mac users will be accustomed to the standard PICT format, which has been common on the platform for ten years or more, whilst Windows users will be accustomed to BMP (sometimes called bitmap images). When it comes to images of predominantly textual pages, there is also the possibility of using Adobe's Portable Document Format (PDF) for viewing in their Acrobat reader. This is certainly an option for converting an original electronic document, but experience shows that capturing from a paper-based source to PDF will result in extremely large file sizes.

An exciting option, currently being employed by the Early English Books online project (EEBO), is the DjVU file format (see **http://www.djvu.com**). This allows for compressions rates of up to 1000:1, and for the delivery of colour images. The format does require a plug-in for the web browser, but this is available for both the Mac and the PC. Again, although the take-up of DjVU outside EEBO has not been high, it is worth considering as an option.

Digitization hardware and software

The final part of the main triad of digital imaging issues is hardware and software. So far the discussion has looked at the breakdown of the image, and the possible resulting file format. It is now time to look at the range of machinery available to accomplish this task – namely the types of scanners and cameras, and what each is best suited for.

Digitization hardware: how does it work?

At the root of most (but not all) image digitization tools is the charge-coupled device or CCD. From the Hubble telescope to the flatbed scanner, this is the basic component that allows us to convert analog to digital. The CCD is actually an analog device with the digitization carried out by an analog-to-digital (A/D) converter. The process uses light-sensitive material on a silicon chip to detect photons (the light emanating or reflecting from the source item), which are recorded electronically in the picture elements or pixels discussed above. One can easily see the CCD in action by looking at a flatbed scanner. As soon as the computer tells the peripheral device to scan (by a prompt issued from the software), a long beam of light will pass under the document projecting light onto its surface (the document being face down on the glass of the scanner). At the same time, this records the reflected light onto the chip of the CCD. Depending on how new the scanner is, it may also employ a prism (de facto in cameras) which separates the light source into red, green, and blue tones (the primary colours used to create RGB images on your monitor). One should also note the emergence of the CMOS (complimentary metal oxide semiconductor) – a rival to the CCD. This is generally a cheaper option but tends to increase the amount of 'noise' in the final image, leading to loss of quality or distortion.

Digitization hardware: some preliminary thoughts

As with so many issues in digitization, there are choices to be made – in this case in the type of hardware one may purchase to perform conversion. This will be dictated by several factors. First there is the type of media one will be digitizing (eg if there are large stocks of microfilms, then one will need access to a microfilm scanner). Then there is the content nature of the source material: is it simply black and white (or bi-tonal), shades of grey (greyscale), or does it retain colour information that is important? Furthermore, before purchasing the equipment, one must consider the working environment of the machine. For example, will it be moved around a lot? Will it be needed to perform predominantly low-level scanning with a quick throughput? Or is it to be used for high-quality scanning where time is not such a pressing issue? Ultimately, of course, one will have to look to the budget available. How much money is there to spend on equipment, bearing in mind the fact that one also has to employ skilled staff, accommodate them, provide ancillary computers to help in the processing and so on?

To assist in this complicated decision-making process, the following basic questions will help in evaluating and selecting particular pieces of hardware:

1   Will the equipment be able to cope with the specific source material in the collection?
2   How easy is the equipment to use?
3   Can one add extra lenses if necessary?
4   What effective resolution and bit-depth can the hardware produce?
5   What dynamic range is offered?
6   In trials, how much noise (random signal variation) is present in the resulting scans? Noise in general terms can be viewed as a distortion or deterioration of the image brought about by a variety of factors. Optical noise can be caused by a lens flare, but thermal noise can be brought on (especially in cameras) by overheating of the internal sensor (thus the longer the exposure time, the worse the problem).
7   Is the scanner TWAIN-compliant? Hardware and software that use TWAIN standards can easily communicate with each other. They employ a

device driver which is installed on the PC and allows software such as Adobe Photoshop to drive the scanner directly.

8 What is the machine's throughput? That is to say, under normal conditions (not the optimum ones used by manufacturers), how long does it take to perform a standard scan?

9 What file formats can one output to? For example, does it allow one to save directly to a non-compressed TIFF, or does it automatically output to a proprietary format?

10 How does the piece of equipment connect to the PC? How easy is it to connect it to the PC, and what cabling system is used (eg via the serial or parallel ports, by SCSI or by memory cards)?

The complexity of this decision-making process drives many to seek solutions elsewhere, out-sourcing their digitization to external agencies (see Chapter 4). These agencies will have built up expertise in digitization, and amassed a stock of the necessary hardware and software. Furthermore, they will have the capital to invest and test the new technologies that are appearing. Nevertheless, even if one does choose to out-source the digitization, it is worthwhile having some familiarity with the range of scanning hardware that may be used for the material.

Contact and non-contact digitization

We have noted at several instances that curatorial concerns may have direct influence on how source material is digitized. For example, handling of a rare and delicate item (such as a manuscript or painting) may be restricted regardless of digitization. One would not be able to run one's finger across an original copy of the Magna Carta, for example. Therefore it is not surprising that certain types of scanning will also be prohibited for conservation reasons. As will be explained below, an example of this is the flatbed scanner, where the source item is laid face down on a plate of glass. Apart from the fact that the bright light from the CCD may be damaging, the surface of the item itself is touching the glass. This is termed *contact digitization*, and for obvious reasons is often prohibited for the handling of rare or fragile items.

The opposite to this is *non-contact digitization*, where no piece of hardware actually touches the source item. The most obvious example of this is the digital camera. Here, the lens of the camera is physically distanced from the item itself. Furthermore, the lighting can be controlled better (relative to the CCD at least) to reduce heat, or to employ extra facilities such as ultraviolet or infrared illumination.

A survey of digitizing hardware

Flatbed scanners

The flatbed scanner is by far the most common piece of equipment available, being almost ubiquitous with any home PC purchase. The scanner has a glass plate onto which the source document is laid face-down. The CCD moves beneath the surface of the glass, recording the reflected light as an array of pixels. Flatbed scanners are both quick and economical to use. They have increased in speed over the last few years and most of them now perform a single pass under the document (whereas older scanners performed a triple pass for red, then blue and finally green). They allow for bi-tonal, greyscale and colour scanning, and are often bundled with their own scanning software and occasionally OCR software. Most flatbed scanners on the market offer a resolution of 600 dpi as base, though some can rise to as high as 1200 dpi (or fall as low as 300 dpi). Standard specification is 24-bit colour (ie eight-bit for each of the three primary colours: red, blue and green), but some scanners now available on the market for reasonable prices claim to offer 36-bit colour and are especially good for digitizing transparencies. Low-end scanners usually offer a dynamic range of between 2.0 and 2.5, but high-end models can go up to 3.4 or 3.9. With very few exceptions, all will allow the user to scan an A4 page (the width is usually 8.5 inches, while the length ranges from 12 to 14 inches). Occasionally, with an extra adapter, the flatbed scanner is suitable for capturing (on a one-by-one basis) 35-mm slides.

Flatbed scanners range dramatically in price from under £100 to up to £1000, but in general a good scanner such as the Hewlett Packard ScanJet 6300C would cost around £300. All-in-one solutions that act as printers, scanners and fax machines are also available, but here the document physically moves through the machine (which is problematic from a conservation perspective), and these tend to have a slower throughput. These all-in-one machines should not be confused with digital capture and sender devices, which in a sense act as Internet-based fax machines allowing documents to be captured and sent across the network without the need for a dedicated PC.

Flatbed scanners capable of handling A3-sized paper are gradually coming onto the market. For example, a top-of-the-range model like the UMAX Mirage II Pro scans documents up to 11.4 inches by 17 inches. These are usually priced at around £2000.

The main disadvantage of the flatbed is that it relies on contact scanning, and is thus unsuitable for rare or valuable material. It also requires the document to be placed flat on the glass, so any curvature of the source material will distort the image.

Sheet-feeders

Sheet-feeders or automatic document feeders (ADFs) are useful if one is faced with large quantities of loose-leaf documents which need processing. Some flatbed scanners provide the option of attaching the feeder to them as an optional peripheral (eg the UMAX Astra 2400), whereas others come with them built in. In general, like with the all-in-one solution noted above, the document is fed through the machine past a stationary CCD. The benefit of this type of scanner is its speed, and one can leave it churning through the documents unattended, with the only limit being the number of pages that can be loaded into the feeder at one time (eg 50 to 100). In reality this proves to be extremely quick – especially if one wishes to perform OCR (optical character recognition) on the text, as the images can be saved and batch processed later – but again, there is the problem that it is unable to deal with fragile or brittle items. Furthermore, there are often limitations on the size of documents that can be processed (usually restricted to around A4).

In terms of cost, an ADF add-on to a standard scanner will often only run to between £100 and £200. However, with dedicated sheet-feeder scanners the price leaps dramatically. For example, the Kodak 3510 production scanner, which can process 40 pages per minute at 300 dpi, costs in the region of £15,000, whilst industrial scanners, such as Kodak's Document Scanner 9500, capable of processing up to 320 pages per minute at 300 dpi, can cost in excess of £60,000. In general 'simplex' scanners (which can only do one side of the page) will cost less than a 'duplex' model (which can scan both sides of the document).

Drum scanners

These are at the top end of the range in terms of price, allowing one to scan in prints and transparencies at very high resolutions (and the highest dynamic range). The drum scanner is so-called because the source document is actually attached to a glass drum. This rotates and the image is read a line at a time by photomultiplier tube technology (not a CCD in this case). The photomultiplier records the reflection of a bright point of light, focused onto the document. Not only do drum scanners allow one to capture reasonably sized documents (eg 12 inches by 17 inches), they offer probably the highest resolution around (up to 12,500 dpi) and can reach a dynamic range of 4.0. However, these scanners are extremely expensive and are rarely found outside a dedicated scanning agency. Desktop drum scanners are available, but top-of-the-range models, such as the Isomet Corporation 405HR Digital Drum Scanner, can cost around £25,000.

Slide scanners

From the outset it should be noted that many flatbed scanners claim to act as slide scanners (for 35-mm slides). To a certain degree this is true, as one can employ a card template fixing the slide in position on the glass, and then simply scan the area of the image. However, there are two problems with this. First, the resolution may be poor (exacerbated by the fact that the surface of the slide is removed – albeit fractionally – from the surface of the glass). Second, digitizing in this way is a slow, laborious process that involves removing the slide, placing the next one in position, altering the scan area (or post-rotating the digital image) depending on whether the image is portrait or landscape, and so on. The sheet-feeders described above unfortunately do not allow one to automatically process 35-mm slides.

Therefore slide scanners, dedicated pieces of hardware for the capture of 35-mm slides or 5-by-4-inch transparencies are often bought as part of the digitizer's toolkit. Low-priced slide scanners ranging from £500 to £1200, such as the Nikon Coolscan 2000, which offers up to 2700 dpi, can process a 35-mm slide every 20 seconds at a three-times-12-bit colour depth (one for each RGB channel). A higher-end model, such as the Nikon LS-4500AF (c £6500) allows for the capturing of much more material: 4-by-5-inch film, 35 mm, 40 mm, 65 mm, 75 mm and 120/220 formats, as well as positive, negative, colour or monochrome. As with everything, the more money one has at one's disposal, the more choice there is.

The resolution of 2700 dpi (or 3000 dpi with the 4500) may seem extremely attractive compared with the 600–1000 dpi that flatbed scanners offer. However, when digitizing slides and other surrogates, the problem of effective resolution comes to the fore. Depending upon the reduction ratio used in the slide, you may actually be getting resolutions of only 200–300 dpi.

Microfilm scanners

Film scanners separate themselves into roll film (standard microfilm) and fiche scanners. The former loads the reel in a similar way to a microfilm reader and then progresses through it, automatically detecting each new frame and scanning the image. When looking at such scanners, it is important to note whether they will accommodate both 16-mm and 35-mm film, and how they cope with positive and negative images. Fiche scanners are similar to sheet-feeders in that they can take a stack of microfiches and process through them (about 50–100 at a time). Microfilm scanners at the low price end can fit onto existing microfilm readers (eg the Nanomach ScreenScan 100-DRP model, c £3500) but most people look towards dedicated scanners using their own optics. For some time now, Mekel Technology Inc have specialized in developing such scanners, producing desktop models like the M520 (roll film, c £26,000) and the M560aps (fiche, c £40,000). At the extreme, the SunRise ProScan is a production-line scanner, costing around £80,000. However, it presents a three-in-one solution allowing for roll film, fiche and aperture card scanning. At its peak it can process around 150 frames per minute at 200 dpi, but at slower speeds it can achieve 600 dpi. When buying such hardware one should note all the possible costs such as a contractual obligation to a service/maintenance agreement, and an up-front fee for training and installation.

Digital cameras

The emergence of the digital camera over the past few years into the mass consumer market has brought this type of equipment to many people's attention. High-street retailers often sell computers aimed at the domestic market bundled with scanners, printers and increasingly a hand-held digital camera. Whilst it is a good thing that this technology is now available to most people at a reasonable price, it has tended to denigrate the role of the digital camera and its popular status in digitizing.

The problem with the digital cameras that come with such 'domestic' packages is that they offer very low resolutions. For example, the Kodak DC 215 only offers 1152 × 864 pixels (though it does provide a digital zoom × 2), which in effect will be about a tenth of what one needs for high-level digitization. Similarly it outputs automatically to JPEG (a lossy compression format described above). Although this will average around £250, making it affordable at the individual level, and it will provide extremely quick throughput, it is unsuitable for a digitization project.

Instead, the large projects such as those running at the National Library of Scotland, the Arnamagnean Institute in Iceland or the British Library, use a high level camera that at minimum will provide an effective resolution of 300–600 dpi, and 24-bit colour. Popular models being used at the moment are the Kontron Progress 3012, which gained considerable publicity from Robinson's favourable descriptions (Robinson, 1993). So much so that the Kontron, costing in excess of £20,000, has been the main stalwart of digitization initiatives (especially of rare manuscript material) throughout the 1990s, offering in effect a dpi of around 600, with 24-bit colour.

Without considering the high price, there are, however, three inherent problems with this type of camera. First, the scan time can be quite long. This means that lighting conditions have to be maintained throughout – a potentially damaging procedure when using warm lighting on rare documents (and increasing the chance of optical noise). Second, they are cumbersome pieces of equipment, often requiring some form of stand or cradle, as well as the PC needed to link to the camera. Third, because of their cost, they tend to be used for high-level digitization only, the natural impulse being to get as high a resolution as possible from the camera, regardless of whether this is appropriate for the project.

The first pioneers in the use of such cameras in libraries during the early nineties came across several difficulties that had to be overcome. For example, in most cases the material they were handling was often rare or fragile, and therefore the scanning process had to accommodate conservation concerns. Most notably this manifested itself in the digitization of books that could not be opened beyond 45 degrees on account of the delicate binding. Cradles had to be designed and built to allow the camera to be placed perpendicular to the page. An example of this can be seen in Figure 3.2 and Figure 3.3 where two possible positions for such a camera are outlined.

In both instances, the operator must ensure perpendicularity between the source document and the camera. Unlike the scanners such as the Minolta and Zeutschel below, digitization cameras tend not to compensate for page curvature. Therefore a number of systems have been developed to help overcome this, ranging from bone handles (to hold the page down) to vacuum plates.

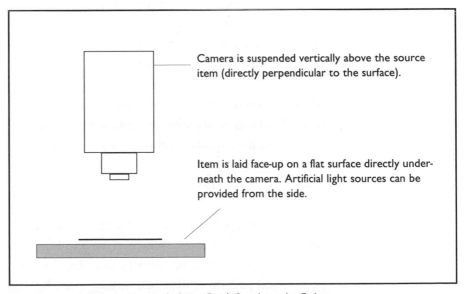

Fig. 3.2   *Camera positioned above flat (often loose-leaf) document*

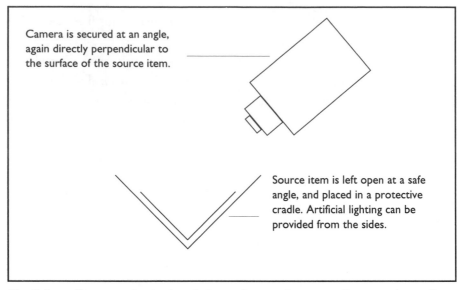

Camera is secured at an angle, again directly perpendicular to the surface of the source item.

Source item is left open at a safe angle, and placed in a protective cradle. Artificial lighting can be provided from the sides.

Fig. 3.3   *Camera maintains its relation to the page by means of a protective cradle*

Oversized document scanners and scanbacks (or digital backs)

One of the major limitations of the digital cameras noted above is their inability to handle large-format documents such as maps, posters, engineering drawings and so on. When you are faced with the problem of scanning large-format sources, there are three possible solutions:

- adopt the internegative approach (described below) – ie photograph the original and digitize the film surrogate at high quality
- purchase or use a scanner that is specifically built to deal with large-format documents (eg A1 or A0)
- employ a piece of hardware known as a scanback.

The internegative approach is explained later, which leaves for now a discussion of dedicated pieces of hardware. When it comes to large-format scanners, it can be said that they generally work best with loose-leaf documents such as drawings and posters, and perform at their best quality when digitizing black-and-white material (although the market also supports overhead bound-volume scanners).

The Vidar TruScan Select scanner, for example, offers 400-dpi black-and-white scanning for A0 documents (c £7000), whilst the Vidar TruScan Titan offers 24-bit colour at 400 dpi (c £13,000). However, both employ a feed mechanism which physically moves the source document through the scanner. This is common in many large-format scanners designed primarily for engineering drawings (ie non-rare material), but would obviously cause some concern in terms of conservation. Good scanners will feed the document through without bending it and also allow the speed of throughput to be controlled, which may allay some fears. Furthermore, the documents themselves (if not too fragile) can be placed in plastic sleeves protecting their surface from the scanner's internal components.

However, one can still think of many documents that could not be processed in such a way – eg extremely fragile material, or bound volumes which can not be dismembered. In this case one needs to look to a large-format open-book scanner. Zeutschel GmbH offer a range of these, starting with their OmniScan 5000/5100 (A2, eight-bit greyscale, 600 dpi), which utilizes a cradle technique, a glass plate to hold down the pages, and offers an automatic electronic image correction of the book curve. At the top of the range is their Omniscan 7000 A0 scanner (E size), which offers 800 dpi, eight-bit greyscale. The stalwart of open-book digitization projects in the UK has been the Minolta PS3000, now replaced by the more recent PS 7000 (**http://www.minoltaeurope.com/**). The latter model scans up to A2 books and 3-D objects face-up at up to 600 dpi in halftone. It also offers sophisticated image editing – eg improved curve correction, centring, centre erasing, image rotation and variable magnification. Large-format open-book scanners are expensive pieces of equipment, though, costing c £25–30,000.

Finally there is the scanback option. Alternatively known as a digital camera back, this is a piece of hardware that fits onto the back of a traditional camera, often into the film plane of existing 4-by-5-inch cameras, giving a pixel array of around 7000 × 6000. The major advantage is that this thereby provides perfect compatibility with the lenses and cameras already available. Not only will this allow one to capture high resolution images, but it also means one can photograph A0 material. However, unless a special cradle is designed (as in Figure 3.3 above for the digital camera), maintaining perpendicularity between the camera and the surface of the source document can be a problem, and unlike with the Zeutschel scanners above there is no automatic correction for page curvature. In their defence, scanbacks are generally much quicker than the digital cameras described above. Examples of such scanbacks are the PowerPhase FX by Phase One, which can offer 48-bit colour and 300 dpi on A0 documents, or the range of models supplied by BetterLight. Scanbacks tend to cost in the region of £10,000.

Digitization software

Software for digital imaging covers three main areas:

- capturing the image
- processing the image
- delivering the image (discussed in Chapter 5).

In the first instance one will need a piece of software that can drive (or at least interface with) the peripheral device used for the scanning (the camera or scanner). The TWAIN solution noted above is one such option that allows for this. In addition the software needs to be able to receive the image from the scanner, but most importantly must be able to control the scanning settings (resolution and bit-depth, to name but two). Most software used for this purpose will allow one to preview the image at an extremely low resolution, allowing fine-tuning of the capture area. An excellent example of this, and probably the most commonly used, is Adobe's Photoshop, which is TWAIN-compliant and provides extensive editing tools. This can be used in conjunction with more specialized pieces of software such as DeBabilizer Pro, which is geared particularly towards colour management. Nevertheless it should be recognized that many pieces of hardware (such as flatbed scanners) will come bundled with a range of imaging software, all of which will cover many of the basic requirements.

One final point to take into consideration when choosing the capturing software is the file formats it will allow one to output to. This can be extremely important, particularly when it comes to creating master images. If, for example, it is felt that all the master images should be saved as TIFFs, then obviously the software used should allow one to do this straight away without going through two or three conversion steps.

Processing (or post-editing) the image can involve many things: cropping, fine-tuning the colour balance, applying filters and so on. Similarly, it will often mean the creation of derivatives. This will be discussed in Chapter 4, but in short 'creating derivatives' might mean converting the TIFF master to a format more suitable for web delivery, such as JPEG or GIF.

The digitization assessment stage

We have now established some basic principles about digital imaging, and seen the range of hardware that can be used for scanning, plus the possible file formats that can be produced. Yet so far this has been very much an exercise in the abstract, and we have not investigated how this would interplay with the matrix developed in Chapter 2. There it was suggested that, once a project had been instigated, and a surrogate and copyright check had been performed, the next stage would be to visit the collection itself and view the material. Up to now it has been argued that this would involve a subject specialist and a conservation expert to see if the project was appropriate and did not pose any risk to the collections. At this point we can now also state that a digitization expert should be on hand. He or she, armed with the above knowledge about digitization hardware, software and file formats, will be able to perform what is termed a *digitization assessment*. The aims of this will be:

- to suggest a 'best digitization procedure' which will meet the aims of the project and satisfy the recommendations of curators and conservation experts
- to establish whether digitization should be from the original material or from a surrogate, and where that digitization should take place (eg in-house or out-sourced)
- to establish the costs of conversion (ie the unit cost for digitizing each item, but not for subsequent work such as cataloguing, delivering etc)
- to establish whether the project should be redefined to make it more viable.

Before we look at an expanded matrix that copes with the digitization assessment, we need to consider two more issues. The first of these is the format of the actual material that will be digitized. Then we will need to clarify the term *internegative* (which has been used already) and the appropriate use of film.

The format of the source material

When it comes to conversion, one is faced with two possible scenarios:

- scanning from the original item
- scanning from a surrogate of the original item.

In both cases the nature of the source item needs to be considered: both the material the digitizer is actually presented with and, in the case of the surrogate, the original item itself. One must concentrate on the physical and content attributes of the item. This analysis should be performed by the digitizer in collaboration with the curators of the material and experts in conservation methods. Only then can the digitization assessment be completed. This is especially true when handling the original item itself, especially if it is rare or fragile. As McIntyre (1998) notes, the potential damage that can be inflicted on a document should not be underestimated:

> It is vital that we consider carefully what risk we might be exposing original material to during any proposed scanning procedure. Collection materials are at risk in any handling situation but when an item is being considered for digital scanning, it is likely to be subjected to more handling than usual . . .

When analysing the item, the most common physical attributes that we need to account for are:

The source item's physical constituency

Paper (matt and gloss), vellum, papyri, microform and other transparencies (eg 35-mm slides), glass, three-dimensional objects (eg artefacts such as pottery, statues, book-bindings) etc.

The physical dimensions of the source item

The actual dimensions of the object are extremely important: ie it is difficult to digitize large maps or posters using conventional scanning equipment, and this may require creating a surrogate (eg a photograph) and scanning from that, or buying in specialized equipment (covered below in the internegative approach).

The physical robustness of the source item

How sturdy is the document? Can it be disbound, or is it so valuable or delicate that it needs to be digitized under strict conditions? For example, Yale's Open Book Project was able to disbind all the material and thus greatly increase the throughput by the digitizers, whilst the Internet Library of Early Journals (ILEJ) project in the UK could not disbind any of the material as it was handling 18th and 19th-century items, thus slowing down the speed of conversion. At the other end of the scale are the requirements of such projects as the manuscript digitization at the British Library, which has to work from the original items, all of them national treasures. This necessitates the use of special cradles to hold the manuscripts and buying in specialized lighting equipment.

In addition to the physical format of the material, the *content* attributes of the document also need to be analysed. The following categories into which one could pigeon-hole source documents are offered, and apply to both original documents and surrogates:

1   Black-and-white (monochrome) documents such as text, woodcuts or lineart.
2   Documents with gradation in tones, either monochrome (ie grey gradations between black and white) or colour. This would cover photographs, transparencies, works of art, manuscripts etc. In the case of photographs one would choose between the negative and the print as to which provides the best source quality.
3   Documents containing halftones with spaced patterns of dots (either monochrome or colour), often used in line engravings and etchings.

Of course many items will contain a mixture of two or more of these. For example, a modern magazine may have colour images interspersed amongst black-and-white text. In this case, you set your sights at retaining the information (ie digitizing) at the highest level needed. For the magazine, then, you would digitize the whole page as colour if the images were considered important (unless you had the time and inclination to separate text from images during the digitization process).

Surrogates v originals and the internegative approach: the use of film

There are four possible scenarios in which the digitizer will have to face film:

1   The collection consists of a good stock of film surrogates which are of sufficient quality, thus negating any need to digitize from the original (should that be possible).

2   To match preservation needs: as noted in Chapter 2, film provides a well-established preservation medium (particularly black-and-white film captured to modern standards) and thus the conservators may state that at some point in the project a film copy needs to be made of the item.

3   It may be perceived that traditional photography poses less of a risk of causing damage to the original item than using digitization equipment. Most high-level digitization cameras can not yet use flash lighting effectively – the best solution at the moment is that being offered by the Scitext Corporation with their Leaf cameras (**http://www.scitex.com/**). Consequently this may require that the item is exposed to direct artificial light for several minutes. In this case the conservators may state that digitization can only be done from the surrogate.

4   It may be impossible actually to capture the item to the required resolution using the digitizing equipment to hand (eg the item may be oversized, such as a map, which will require an initial photograph or transparency to be taken which can then be digitized).

We would usually state that options 2–4 above were adopting an internegative approach. This is because, in between the original item and the digital file, a surrogate is taken for the sole purpose of completing the aims of the digital project.

When it comes to option 2, where you need to create a recognized preservation film copy, there is a further question that needs to be asked. Should the project photograph the source material first (eg to microfilm) and then digitize from that, or should digital images be created directly from source and then a film copy made from them (known as COM, which stands for computer output microfilm)? In other words should the project film first, or scan first?

The debate over this has continued for some time now. The most comprehensive review of the potential of COM was performed by the Cornell Digital Microfilm Conversion Project (see Kenney, 1997). This was a sister project to Yale's Open Book initiative, as both were involved in creating images of 19th-century brittle books. The COM project investigated the quality and cost-effectiveness of the scan first and then output to microfilm approach, as opposed to filming first and then scanning. They concluded that

> COM created from 600 dpi 1-bit images can exceed ANSI/AIIM microfilm standards. Furthermore the digital images were of a higher standard if captured directly from the source material as opposed to scanning from microfilm. The costs associated with scanning first appear to be less than those incurred in the film first approach.

However, the study also pointed out that:

> . . . the decision to go with one approach over the other [film first or scan first] will depend on a range of variables associated with the attributes of the original, institutional capabilities, and the availability of appropriate imaging products and services.

For example, in Australia's Ferguson Project (Webb, 1996) the process outlined by Cornell for COM was balanced with the film first and scan second approach of such projects as Yale's Open Book initiative and the latter was adopted (though Webb notes that this also led to considerable difficulties).

To summarize the findings of the current discussions, it would appear that digitizing first and then outputting to microfilm can produce significantly better results, as noted above, especially when the project will involve later OCRing of text. On the other hand, microfilming first (with the knowledge that the film is to be subsequently digitized) can be a much cheaper process, and probably more manageable using most traditional photographic studios (ie they have the capability to create the film and this can then be sent out to external digitizing agencies).

What does this mean for the digitization assessment?

Putting this together, we can begin to see the important implications that the nature of the source material will have for the digitization process adopted. In terms of the varying problems that will be presented, the digitizer may have to confront:

- bi-tonal (monochrome) images
- greyscale (continuous tone) images
- and colour (continuous tone) images.

In addition he or she will be handling original items (some extremely rare or fragile) and surrogates.

The visit to the collection should then be considered as essential, as it will illustrate which of these problems the project will present. The digitization expert needs to consider the aims of the project, and notably whether the project is trying to meet preservation needs, and if so, whether a film copy will be needed. Alternatively, is the project simply attempting to satisfy access needs? Then perhaps only low-quality images will be required – or more probably, high-quality digital images will be taken and low-quality derivatives created at a later stage. The digitization expert, as part of the assessment, would then formulate a proposed *digitization method* that will satisfy the aims of the project and the concerns of the curators, and take into account the resulting costs and throughput. At this point, also, all the surrogates that will be needed (if any) should be clearly catalogued, and a decision will need to be made as to what part of the digitization will be performed in-house as opposed to being outsourced.

The final part of the digitization assessment will be some initial recommendations about the resolutions and bit-depths to be employed during the proposed conversion. As yet this chapter has not attempted to address this problem, mainly because there is really no simple answer. Frey and Reilley (1999, 1) point out in a recent study of this area:

> There are no guidelines or accepted standards for determining the level of image quality required in the creation of digital image databases for photographic collections.

Therefore, if there are no obvious standards or targets in place, how can one decide upon exact specifications for scanning? Some formulae which attempt to calculate scanning resolutions automatically have been derived in the past, it has to be said, and are still occasionally used. Granger et al (1996) reproduced a standard formula in their overview:

> Suggested scanning resolution = lines per inch (or original) $\times$ 1.4 $\times$ (desired size/size of original)

Although many experienced digitizers may query whether such a formula can work (using a constant of 1.4, for example, goes against the grain of the inconsistent nature of digitization), this formula does throw up some fairly acceptable results recommending such rates as:

- 35-mm slides to be scanned at c 2900 dpi
- 5-by-4-inch transparencies at c 690 dpi
- c A4 sheets at 300 dpi.

However, this formula has an important caveat. These resolutions are meant to guarantee 'good quality printing up to A3 in size'. This method is thus intended to satisfy one purpose, and one purpose only: printing. What if we wished to scan an item so that it could satisfy many purposes, or so that we could derive files from it that could be used in various applications? As Williams (1998) notes, 'Ideally we should provide one scan to fit all purposes'.

Franziska Frey (1997) explains that 'a growing consensus within the preservation community is that a number of image files must be created for every photograph to meet a range of uses.' This point will be discussed further in Chapter 4, but for now it is worth bearing in mind that a digital master can be used to produce all kinds of derivatives which will be applicable to different scenarios. Frey goes on to outline a set of standards for three example files that would be appropriate for wider access (see Table 3.1).

Table 3.1

The digital image is used only as a visual reference image in an electronic database.	• low quality • thumbnails less than 250 pixels (long edge) • on-screen viewing set to 480 × 640 • colour reproduction not critical • compression allowed.
The digital image is used for reproduction.	• desired reproduction needs to be clearly defined, but example of 8 × 10-inch hard copy at 300 dpi, needs only a 2400 × 3000 pixel file • colour mapping essential.
The digital image represents a 'replacement' of the original in terms of spatial and tonal information content.	• pixel levels vary from original to original • eight-bit colour not adequate for future needs.

These should be looked on as simple generic guidelines and cannot be viewed as an accurate forecast of the digitizing standards for all projects of a similar nature. As noted above, there are too many variables which may come into play differentiating between seemingly similar types of source documents or different projects. A project that is digitizing purely and simply for ephemeral web delivery may consider it overkill to go for 600 dpi. Conversely, a venture that is concerned with creating high-quality images would not wish to store everything in JPEG format at 100 dpi. An international survey of published reports from current digital projects shows a wide discrepancy in practices world-wide. Therefore, one can only attempt to present suggestions for resolutions and bit-depths which adhere to the most commonly accepted recommendations. These are presented below, but rest on the assumption that the project is interested in creating master images from which derivatives (both digital and print) are to be created.

This concept of the *master image* is worth teasing out further. Frey and Reilly (1999, 3) offer the following definitions:

> The digital master is the file that is archived. It represents the highest quality file that has been digitized. Since this is the information that is supposed to survive and be taken into the future, the main issues in creating the digital master relate to longevity and quality.
>
> The derivatives are the files for daily use. Speed of access and transmission and suitability for certain purposes are the main issues to consider in the creation of derivative files.

The recommended procedure for these master images would be:

1   Images should be digitized to the highest possible standard, and the resulting files should be saved as uncompressed TIFF images (Intel byte order), or Group 4 compressed TIFFs for bi-tonal documents.
2   In terms of resolutions the minimum effective level should be set to 300 dpi, but ideally it should be 600 dpi.
3   All colour images should be scanned at 24 bits, greyscale images at eight bits, and bi-tonal at eight bits (but probably delivering at one bit).
4   Interpolation should be avoided at all costs.

To summarize then, during the digitization assessment stage the imaging expert will visit the collection, along with the subject and conservation expert(s). He/she will study the format and content of the items. Bearing in mind the project aims he/she will suggest a digitization method outlining the type of hardware to be used, the need for surrogates, if any of the conversion is to be outsourced, and finally the resolutions and bit-depths that should be used for each item (or category of items) in the collection.

Feasibility: the final piece of the matrix

Armed with the knowledge from the digitization assessment, we are now in a position to complete the matrix that we began in Chapter 2. So far, the project has been instigated, checked and assessed in terms of what benefits it will produce under the headings increasing access, meeting preservation needs, and matching institutional strategies. Now, with the input of the digitization expert who has provided a proposed digitization method, we are in a position to ask whether the project is actually feasible or not. It is not suggested that this would be a simple yes or no answer (ie either the project goes ahead or does not), but instead, as with the other categories, a way of prioritizing projects in terms of how easily they might be completed, and pointing out where more work needs to be done. Input at this stage will come from all areas, according to the types of questions that need to be asked. In essence, though, the aim here is to see whether there is sufficient hardware, software and expertise available to complete the project, bearing in mind the constraints imposed by time and money. In addition, it should also be noted whether the project would involve considerable additional work (such as cataloguing) for it to be successful. To complete the matrix, then, we could add the checklist shown in Figure 3.4.

The observant reader will have noted that Figure 3.4 contains a section for entering the cost of digitization. This will be discussed in the next chapter, but for now one could imagine entering a cost range (ie less than £5000; between £5000 and £10,000; £10–20,000 etc). Once this has been done, the managers of the project (or more likely a number of projects), will be in a position to prioritize collections, and to state whether they can go ahead or not.

An example of prioritization

To conclude this chapter, let us look at another hypothetical situation involving three typical collections and, using the matrix built up over the past three chapters and the knowledge now acquired about digitization, attempt to prioritize them.

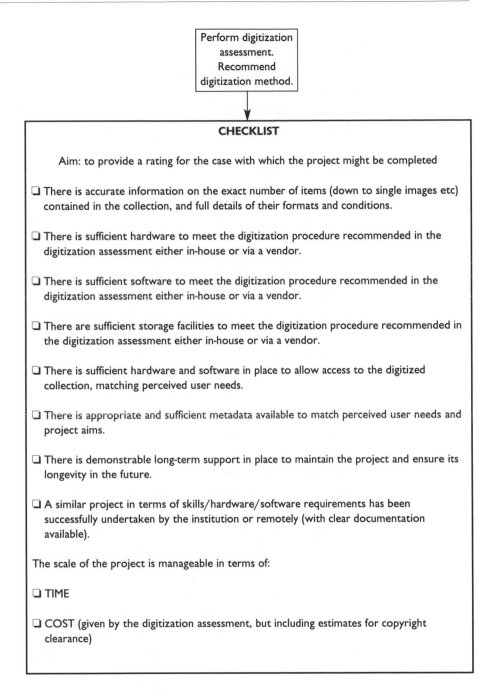

Perform digitization assessment. Recommend digitization method.

CHECKLIST

Aim: to provide a rating for the case with which the project might be completed

❏ There is accurate information on the exact number of items (down to single images etc) contained in the collection, and full details of their formats and conditions.

❏ There is sufficient hardware to meet the digitization procedure recommended in the digitization assessment either in-house or via a vendor.

❏ There is sufficient software to meet the digitization procedure recommended in the digitization assessment either in-house or via a vendor.

❏ There are sufficient storage facilities to meet the digitization procedure recommended in the digitization assessment either in-house or via a vendor.

❏ There is sufficient hardware and software in place to allow access to the digitized collection, matching perceived user needs.

❏ There is appropriate and sufficient metadata available to match perceived user needs and project aims.

❏ There is demonstrable long-term support in place to maintain the project and ensure its longevity in the future.

❏ A similar project in terms of skills/hardware/software requirements has been successfully undertaken by the institution or remotely (with clear documentation available).

The scale of the project is manageable in terms of:

❏ TIME

❏ COST (given by the digitization assessment, but including estimates for copyright clearance)

Fig. 3.4 *Feasibility checklist*

Example

The University of Wessex is interested in pursuing a series of digitization projects, and has canvassed its librarians, curators and academics about which collections of projects they would recommend. Having circulated all interested parties with the questionnaire (see Appendix B), they have received the following submissions:

Hardy photographs

Description: 900 photographs covering the period of Thomas Hardy's life around 1900, containing pictures of the writer and of Wessex. All are in high demand from Hardy scholars and local historians. Some surrogates exist but not a substantial amount. The items are contained in 15 photographic albums, which are in a delicate state but can be opened. The photographs themselves are in most cases in a fragile state and must be handled with extreme care. A catalogue exists to the item level, with a brief description of the contents of each picture and its provenance.

Kewell manuscripts

Description: two medieval manuscripts from the 11th century containing unique Anglo-Norman literary texts. In particular, five folios contain illuminated miniatures depicting life under the Norman yoke. Both manuscripts are unique, both have been microfilmed in full (as recently as 1976), colour slides also exist for the five miniatures, and their full contents are extensively catalogued in several publications. Though unique they are in good condition and can be opened without conservation risk. Total number of folios: 476, all of them c A4 in size.

The Matthews collection

Description: Sir John Matthews was one of the primary British politicians involved in the Anglo-Irish War of the 1920s. His collection is housed in the Social Sciences Library and consists of 34 boxes, uncatalogued beyond a general finding aid and containing hundreds of letters (hand-written and typescript), diaries, photographs, maps, newspapers etc from the time of the conflict up to Matthews' death in 1942. However, the exact number of items is not known at the moment. Some of the material is in poor condition, and none of it has been microfilmed to anyone's knowledge.

Taking these three projects through the decision matrix, we could see that none of them have a full range of surrogates available that would satisfy all user needs. When it comes to copyright there are notable problems with two of the collections: Hardy and Matthews.

First, let us consider the Matthews collection. Because it is dated from the mid-part of the 20th century, there would be numerous problems in locating and agreeing the rights to reproduce. Even if the Matthews estate agreed to this automatically, you would still have to chase up (or ignore at your peril) material by third parties. Furthermore, the indication that the collection is uncatalogued should ring alarm bells. To assess fully and select items from the collection, one would need some indication of the number of documents, their type (which would probably not be contained in the general finding aid), condition, content and so on. Therefore, if the University of Wessex was limited in its funding, it would probably put the Matthews collection to one side for the time being, bearing in mind the copyright problems, and the fact that money would need to be secured for a major cataloguing exercise.

Second, there are the Hardy photographs. These may also present some copyright problems, as the rights on the images would rest with the photographer's executor. The UK law on photography is problematic, but in short, material is considered as being in copyright for 70 years after the date of creation if the photos were made before June 1957 (which these were). Therefore, assuming that the photographs making up this collection were from before 1930, then they would be out of copyright. On the other hand, no copyright problems exist for the Kewell manuscripts on account of their date, or the surrogates taken from them, as these were done by the university's reprographics studio.

A visit to each of the latter collections (Hardy and Kewell) would allow the subject expert, the conservator and the digitizer (who could in theory all be the same person) to make some more substantial recommendations. These might include:

1   As both items are rare, then preservation is a concern. The Kewell manuscripts have been microfilmed already but film copies would need to be made of the full Hardy collection if preservation goals are to be met.

2   Non-contact scanning is required.
3   There is no colour information needed in the Hardy collection, but the illuminations from the Anglo-Norman collection will need to be digitized at high-quality colour levels.
4   For both collections it would be wise to have master images of the highest possible quality plus access images for the web.
5   No further cataloguing is needed.

The digitization assessment might include the following recommendations:

1   Hardy photographs: make surrogates of all the material if preservation is truly a project aim. These would then be digitized at eight-bit greyscale, 600 dpi, by a flatbed scanner; or digitization could take place using a high-quality camera with film output from the digital file (probably through an external agency).
2   Kewell manuscripts: scan directly from the manuscript using a non-contact scanner at 24-bit colour, 600 dpi. The option of using the microfilm and colour surrogates would mean that:

   • part of the collection would be in monochrome
   • the quality would be lower as the surrogates, by definition, would not be of as good a quality as the original.

Faced with the possibility of choosing between them, the decision matrix would indicate that both projects would score highly under the categories of increasing access and institutional strategies. However, the Hardy photographs would also greatly contribute towards preservation as the source items themselves are under threat. Using the feasibility checklist, one finds that both collections are manageable at low cost and using reasonably affordable equipment (the most expensive being the digital camera). Other things being equal, then, it would probably be recommended that the Hardy project should take the higher priority on the grounds of preservation.

Chapter summary

The aim of this chapter was to present the technical overview of digitization, and then to look at how this will affect our earlier discussions on the assessment and prioritization of collections. In particular it looked at:

- dpi, bit–depths, compression and file formats
- a range of digitization hardware and software
- the digitization assessment stage
- an example of prioritizing a collection.

4 | What are the next steps? Preparation and digitization

Introduction

So far we have looked at some of the initial stages involved in a digital imaging project – in particular the importance of assessing and prioritizing projects – and completed this with a discussion of the initial digitization assessment, armed with knowledge about the technicalities behind the conversion process (such as file formats, resolutions and so on). If we are now to follow the life-cycle of the digitization project, as outlined at the end of Chapter 1, the next steps to be considered are the preparation of the material, and of course their actual digitization. These two areas form the focus of this chapter.

Preparation

Let us begin with the often neglected area of preparation. The aim of this stage is to make sure that all the material needed by the digitization team to complete the project actually reaches them. The assessment and selection stage outlined in the previous chapter will, as part of the process, list the exact items that should go into the digital collection. In turn this will indicate the following:

- if any items needed to complete the project are actually missing, or are in such a poor condition that they should be considered unavailable
- which items are not available for digitization for conservation reasons (eg they are too fragile or are oversized).

In both scenarios workable solutions will need to be found at the preparation stage. These may include locating and securing alternative copies, or in the latter case creating film surrogates for subsequent scanning (the internegative approach mentioned earlier). In addition, it is very possible that the objects for digitization will have to be moved to the location of the digitization equipment. This may only be a matter of moving the material along a corridor or to another building, but in extreme cases it could mean moving it to another city or country. In this instance, at the preparation stage, such matters as packaging, insurance and transport will need to be arranged.

In-house and outsourcing

The above comments lead naturally to the issue of where the scanning is actually being performed: either *in-house* or through *outsourcing*. In a sense, these are very easy terms to define. They are used to reflect where the digitization process takes place, partly in terms of its physical location, but also reflecting who is performing the digitization. The term *in-house* implies firstly that the material is captured somewhere within the premises of the institution. Most importantly, however, it also implies that the onus on supplying the hardware and software, trained personnel and overheads is covered by the host institution internally. Even if the digitization does not take place in the exact location where the collection is usually held (eg the collection is moved to the institution's photographic unit or digitization centre), it is still defined as taking place in-house.

On the other hand *outsourcing* means entering into a contract of some sort with an agency external to the institution to undertake the digitization. In most cases this means paying a dedicated digitization agency to receive the material, convert it and return the originals with the required digital files. The complexity of the agreement one enters into will vary considerably, of course, but outsourcing can be seen as reflecting an undertaking by a body or bodies not directly under the control of the institution. Occasionally, a third party or brokering agency can be used to conduct all the arrangements with the digitization agency. This can be extremely efficient as it allows this third party to perform continual assessments of the performance of external agencies, comparing them and selecting the most cost-effective. Even if the digitization unit employed actually has to come to the host institution to convert the material (eg security reasons may prohibit the movement of rare and valuable material), this would still be termed outsourcing – in other words, one is still paying to bring in external staff, equipment and expertise.

The reasons for choosing one option over the other are varied. The advantages of the in-house scenario are that one will be able to maintain full curatorial control over the material as it is digitized, allowing conservators to observe the process throughout. Usually it is less of a security risk, as the material will probably be moved over a shorter distance, which could imply cost savings in insurance and transport. Furthermore, preparation of the material to ensure that it can be moved safely will be reduced. When it comes to the conversion stage, one will have direct control, quickly seeing the results of different types of scanning and the effects they have on the final deliverable object. This in turn will allow one to define standards and procedures as the project develops, rather than having to state them up-front (as one would have to do if entering into a contract with an external agency).

Furthermore, the human factor in this should not be ignored. In-house scanning will contribute to the expertise base that the institution can draw on in the future. Staff will receive training in different scanning techniques, which can later be used in other projects. This will also contribute to the stock of hardware and software, and, of course, experience in using both.

In-house digitization, on the other hand, does have some notable disadvantages. There is the need to cover the cost of the equipment and software, the training for the staff, and accommodation for the conversion team. The 'ramp-up' time to starting the project will be drawn out at first, as the staff may have to become familiar with the equipment, the material and the processes. Overall, though, the flexibility inherent in performing digitization in-house will mean that the unit cost per image is very hard to establish early on.

Outsourcing the digitization, however, allows one to draw on the established expertise and hardware of commercial companies set up to engage in the conversion of material. They will usually be able to deliver the order with a quick turnaround, and importantly will have the money to invest in new equipment as old cameras, scanners and techniques become redundant. Specialized agencies are available with high-level expertise in such things as microfilm scanning, digitization of 35-mm slides or bulk conversion of printed material. Overall they will offer extremely attractive rates (the unit cost per image of conversion), which will often be much lower than for scanning the material in-house. This is understandable as the project will not have to cover overheads, pay wages or update equipment. Yet outsourcing, by definition, means that the material will at some stage be placed in the hands of staff not directly under the institution's jurisdiction. In other words one will hand over control during the conversion process to a third party – a state of affairs which can be of concern especially when rare or unique items are being handled. Furthermore, outsourcing involves entering into a contract with the agency. To do this satisfactorily, one will need to consider such matters as who retains rights over the digital images, what is the fall-back position should the agency not fulfil its side of the agreement, and so on.

The digitization workflow

Once the material has been prepared and transported, it will then be in the hands of the digitizer (either in-house or outsourced) and the task now is to perform the actual conversion. The rest of this chapter looks at a possible workflow of how this may take place, but before proceeding to this it is worthwhile looking at a real-life example. The following describes a routine operation by the digital photographer Julius Smit, working on the University of Oxford's Celtic and Medieval Manuscript Project.

Example: The digitizer's tale

In order to facilitate the digital imaging of bound manuscripts, a lightweight yet sturdy cradle has been designed to allow each manuscript to sit comfortably whilst being subjected to periods of digital scanning.

Manuscripts are scanned at an angle of 45 degrees, as this allows for the manuscript to be opened at a safe angle of between 90 and 100 degrees. Rectos are scanned first, and then the manuscript is turned around, allowing for the versos to be scanned. Various holding devices (bone folders, weights and polythene tapes with velcro attachments to the sides of the cradle) are used to allow for the safe and sympathetic holding in place of each page, whether the material is of paper, vellum or parchment. It is hoped that the future use of a vacuum wedge placed behind each scanned page will dispense with a variety of holding devices.

Heat and light are regarded as the great enemies of archival material. Digital scanning can be seen not only as a method of preservation but also as a tool of dissemination of information. As a technical process, scanning utilizes photographic principles in its capture process, and of course light and optics play their respective parts.

A 4 × 5 Sinar camera is used with a Dicomed scanning back, which allows for the creation of scanned images with a resolution of up to 6000 × 7520 pixels. Thus a page width of 10 inches would create an image of 600 dpi. Working at 100% resolution does give rise to comparatively long scanning times and the subsequent creation of large computer files. As an example, a page measuring 8 inches by 11 inches, can give rise to a 120-Mb file at 6000 × 7520 pixels with an approximate scanning time of four minutes.

The use of flicker-free high-frequency fluorescent lighting tubes allows for the continual lighting of the object. Three lamps are used in each lighting unit (one unit standing on each side of the cradle). A low heat output of 40 W, whilst only consuming 10 W, is generated by each lamp. Cowls are fitted to the lighting units to allow the operator to close the lights down whilst preparing the next page for scanning.

Before a page is scanned at full resolution, a preview image is created using Imaginator software. Whilst the page is lit at full lighting exposure, focusing is done manually on the camera at a full aperture of f5.6. After focusing, an aperture of between f8 and f11 is used to allow for good depth of field. Five pages are usually scanned in succession before focusing needs to be repeated. Once the manuscript has been set up on the cradle, which can take up to 10–15 minutes, the only time-consuming work is that of setting up each new page for scanning. Depending on the type of material, and its inherent problems, this can take from one-and-a-half to two minutes.

A common problem encountered in the scanning of parchment is cockling. Holding down cockled pages with a variety of implements borders very much on an art form! A good depth of field is required in this case to allow for 'pockets' of varying planes. However, it should be noted here that it is important to remain faithful to the image quality. A smaller lens opening at the same scanning time will produce a much denser image. The answer may well be a longer scanning time. However, this means a longer exposure to light. It is at this stage that the operator's skill and knowledge, not only of computers and photography, but also of archival material, its properties and handling, will come into play.

Each scan is given a unique file reference before scanning begins. Once the scanning back hard disk is full, images are subsequently downloaded to the system disk. At the end of each day, the collection of scanned images is further downloaded to a hierarchical file server (HFS). At a later stage, images are retrieved from the HFS for post-processing, which can include the titling, copyright notice and provision of scale on each image before it is finally mounted on the web.

Julius Smit

Camera Operator, Celtic and Medieval Manuscripts Imaging Project, University of Oxford

Many of the technical details listed in the above example may seem unfamiliar to some readers but this should not cause undue concern. Importantly, the main points to note are:

- the need for specialized equipment – cradles, bone folders, lighting
- the ever-present concerns regarding conservation
- the technical expertise needed to complete the job
- the lengthy process that is involved.

In other words, the above example illustrates that for most digitization it is not simply a matter of pointing and clicking. There is a lengthy process involved in the preparation of the material and in the capture itself. For example, although Smit does not outline it in his explanation, the project in question was one of the first to report problems with lighting brought about by a need (a few years ago) to subject the manuscripts to a five-minute scan time. The light and heat generated actually inflicted a 0.1% shrinkage on the manuscript size – a factor which had to be remedied by the use of cold lighting to allay the fears of the conservators.

When it comes to actually taking the image, Smit notes that the first step is to take a preview. This allows the camera operator to set the focus accurately (which needs to be reset after a few scans), but above all the aim is to 'remain faithful to the image quality'.

With this real-life example in mind, one can begin to tease out the processes involved in the actual digitization of source material. Once the material is received by the digitizers, they will begin to enact the proposals of the digitization assessment performed at the earlier stage. Starting with the proposed digitization method, they will take some sample images to help calibrate the scanning equipment in order to achieve the required quality. In the workflow this is often termed *benchmarking* and is explained in detail later. Once the settings have been established, then the digitization of the images can take place. During this process the original conversion methodology proposed may of course need to be reviewed.

Bringing this together, we suggest that a possible workflow for the actual digitization process would be as follows. Material is received by the digitizer and prepared for digitization (including the setting up of the camera, lights, cradle if necessary, and so on). The proposals of the digitization assessment are put in place. Sample shots are taken for benchmarking, which will allow the camera operator and other experts to calibrate the settings on the hardware and software to achieve the desired results. A preview is taken of the object and then the material is scanned. At regular intervals (and certainly after the first time) a quality assurance check is performed on the digital files. If the images prove unacceptable then one can return to the calibration stage and change the settings, or possibly apply some post-editing processes to compensate for any problems that have appeared in the conversion stage (eg applying filters to adjust colour or light controls, or to automatically cropping images to remove redundant surrounding material). Print or digital derivatives can be created from the master files at an appropriate time. If all is satisfactory, all the electronic files are saved and backed-up according to the institution's archiving policy.

Before defining the digitization workflow, however, it is worth exploring in more detail a few points raised above. Three terms, most notably, have been mentioned in passing that need further elaboration: namely benchmarking, quality assurance, and creating derivatives.

Benchmarking and quality assurance (QA)

Benchmarking can be defined as the process undertaken at the beginning of a digitization project that attempts to set the levels used in the capture process to ensure that the most *significant* information is captured, by setting the resolution or bit-depth correctly. This is different from *quality assurance* which is a post-process check to see if the decisions made earlier were the right ones.

Benchmarking will be a dual process. It will involve not only a study of the source document itself, but also some sample digital shots taking into account the original suggestions at the digitization assessment stage. For these to be successful, however, the benchmarker must have, or have access to:

- full knowledge of the main attributes of the source document (eg its size, what is important in the document and so on)
- recognition of present and future user needs.

The aim of the benchmarking stage is to allow the digitizer:

- to make a final decision about the technical specifications for the digitization (in terms of resolution, sampling rates etc), reconfirming or bringing into question any decisions made at the assessment and selection and digitization assessment stages
- to formally establish hardware and software needs for the project.

If the digitization is to be performed externally, the benchmarking stage will also produce a set of strict requirements against which vendor claims can be judged, and the decision as to which outsourcing agency should be used. Such hard-and-fast facts are essential for dealing with an external contractor.

Once all these have been established, the digitizer will be able to begin to test and calibrate the machines used for conversion, based on the findings of the benchmarking stage. In turn this will provide an accurate idea of how long the digitization will actually take. The most obvious problem with benchmarking is ascertaining what level of capture is satisfactory – ie for present and future needs. Kenney and Chapman (1996b, 7), advocate a 'full informational capture' policy 'ensuring that all significant information contained in the source document is fully represented'. Elsewhere (Kenney and Chapman, 1996a) they elaborate on this by stating that:

> The 'full informational capture' approach to digital conversion is designed to ensure high quality and functionality while minimizing costs. The objective is not to scan at the highest resolution and bit depth possible, but to match the conversion process to the informational content of the original – no more, no less. At some point, for instance, continuing to increase resolution will not result in any appreciable gain in image quality, only a larger file size.

Yet what is the significant information one needs to capture? For text it might be judged as being the smallest letter or symbol that the reader needs to see. In printed books this is often to be found in the footnotes, but in maps the object might be an individual cartographic symbol. In manuscripts it could be down to distinguishing between textures (eg hair and flesh) of the vellum. In photographs or pictures it could be a number of things depending upon the user. The significant detail, then, is often in the eye of the beholder.

The types of things one may wish to look for to pick up for gauging significant factors would include:

- the size and dimensions of the document (width by height in inches)
- size of the details (eg the smallest character or icon)
- medium specific details, such as the type of paper or surface, the writing tool used (pencil, pen, brush and so on)
- the appearance of illustrations
- the range and variety of tones and colours in the document.

Who, though, is experienced enough to answer such questions? When it comes to benchmarking and calibrating machines, James Reilly, Director of the Image Permanence Institute, describes a strategy of 'knowing and loving your documents' (Kenney and Chapman, 1996a). He advocates choosing a representative sample of items and, in consultation with those with curatorial responsibility, identifying key features that are critical to the documents' meaning. Once again, then, it is clear that a successful digitization project requires a combination of curatorial/subject knowledge *and* technical expertise. As Kenney and Chapman (1996b, 26) note:

> Determining what constitutes essential detail is a subjective decision that should be made by those with curatorial responsibility and a good understanding of the nature and significance of the material. Those with a trained eye should consider the attributes of the document itself as well as the potential uses the researchers will make of its informational content.

The benchmarking process, therefore, might be linked to existing expertise in conservation, preservation and reader requirements (ie within the library/curator sector). Equally important, such expertise needs to be on hand to deal with the differing demands of each document. It is noticeable, for example, that many non-digital source materials, such as manuscripts, microfilms etc, contain items collected together that are not homogeneous. A single microfilm reel may contain straightforward images of a printed text, but also a collection of images from an illuminated manuscript. By having expertise to hand one can ensure that the questions that often arise during benchmarking can be quickly answered.

Let us say, then, that a document has been studied by the digitizer and the curator, and that both have drawn up a list of significant features that need to be captured and visible in the resulting digital image. They may, for example, state that when looking at a document the end-user will need to read all the text contained therein, right down to smallest type size. Similarly, if the item is a photograph or a picture, the assessors may judge that it is essential that the end-user be presented with accurate colour representations and gradation in tones. When benchmarking, then, the digitizer will be attempting to satisfy all such requests.

Testing whether one has been successful or not will rely mainly on common sense – for example, in terms of printed material you can either read the text or you cannot. However, more elaborate systems have been developed that involve manual interpretation using the naked eye, a loupe or microscopes, and more automated processes. In the example of the printed text, for example, a quality index system is often advocated based on previous guidelines for microfilming.

Yet overall there will be an element of both subjective and objective analysis. Subjective evaluations usually come first – ie digitizers can actually see on their computer monitors whether the image produced passes the most basic of criteria. They can then move to more objective tests. A pioneering study in this area was conducted by the Research Libraries Group Technical Images Test Project (started in 1992) (see **http://www.rlg.org/pub.html** or **http://www.rlg.ac.uk/ pub.html** for various publications on this and other RLG projects). This was followed by Kenney and Chapman's *Digital imaging for libraries and archives* (Kenney and Chapman, 1996b, 7-34), and more recently by Frey and Reilly (1999). All of these advocated a comprehensive system for checking the photographs, advocating the use of various targets to test different factors (eg the RIT Alphanumeric Resolution Test Object for bi-tonal images or the Modulation Transfer Function for testing detail and resolution). Similarly, other projects point to successful use of colour management systems (CMS) which allow one to adjust colour balances in the digital file compared (manually or automatically) with a selected test target. In a sense all of these are tools to assist the benchmarker in coming up with the correct digitization methods, which can also be utilized in later quality assurance checks.

The above suggestions for benchmarking are entirely valid and form an extremely useful base. However, it should be stressed that the most important factor is that of experience. Regardless of what the more scientific approaches to benchmarking indicate, one is ultimately producing digital images which will be judged by what the user can see, what they can print and so on. As Frey and Reilly (1999, 17) note:

> This does not mean that scanning is done entirely 'by the numbers', because an operator will still be needed to decide when to consciously intervene to improve the subjective quality of the image.

Furthermore, it is widely recognized that no benchmarking can be truly accurate, as nearly every collection encountered will have considerable variation within it; so extensive analysis of a single image may be inappropriate for all the material in the collection. Following this argument it can be said that many practitioners of digitization (notably in the UK) argue that the types of checks outlined above can be viewed as overkill, and could mistakenly convey a sense of scientific exactitude in a field which in reality contains numerous technical variables and differing user requirements.

Once completed, benchmarking will allow digitizers to calibrate their machines and begin to capture the material to meet the desired standards. It is at this stage that quality assurance (QA) checks should be introduced. These will be performed after the digitization has taken place (or more sensibly after *some* of the digitization has taken place). Experience has shown that it is absolutely imperative that all digitization undergoes a series of QA analyses at various stages, regardless of whether the material has been produced in-house or by an outside vendor. Importantly also, one has to be certain that the machine on which one is performing the QA checks, and most notably the monitor, has been set up properly. As Williams (1998) notes:

> It cannot be emphasised strongly enough that any computer used for quality assessment/assurance (QA) of images must be properly set-up and calibrated – this includes any software used for QA and the room in which the QA will be carried out.

Simply put, QA will involve looking at the digital images that have been produced to check that they are of the desired standard and are complete in their expected coverage.

Bearing in mind limits on time and finances, many projects adopt some form of sampling in order to reduce the costs of this process – eg only 10% of digital images may be checked. Ideally, though, quality assurance should be performed on all master images and also in any derivatives, with each step being fully documented. Again, however, one needs to ask what one should be looking for at this stage. In a sense it is generally a process of checking that the images meet the requirements set out in the benchmarking stage – in other words, that the resolutions, bit-depths, tonal values, colours and so on are satisfactory, and that the significant details noted earlier are being represented. Furthermore, now that a concerted program of digitization has taken place, one must check that the quality has been maintained throughout. For example, it may be discovered that the cameras used for digitization should have been recalibrated mid-way through the process. The overall return should be checked for other details such as file name integrity, completeness of job and overall satisfaction. Not only does this cover such micro-details as missing pixels or lines, the appearance of distortion on the image, or indeed unrequested cropping or misorientation of the image; it also refers to the macro-problem of missing images (which can occur, for example, if the digitizer has accidentally turned over two pages of a journal instead of one). For anyone coming to digitization from the world of microfilming, these problems and checks will seem all too familiar.

In more general terms, benchmarking and QA can be assisted by concentrating on some of the categories below. Once again, it needs to be stressed that such checks can only be effectively carried out if the person has adequate knowledge of the original item in terms of the type of material that is or was being digitized, its dimensions, the size of significant details (icons, text), the tones and colour ranges and so on. With this in mind, then, the person charged with checking the digital files could ask the following questions:

1   General details
   • Is the job complete – ie are there signs of any images missing?
   • Have the file naming conventions been adhered to?
2   Image mode
   • Have all images been captured in the correct mode (eg have colour images been captured as colour files etc)?
   • Are the returned images in the correct file formats, and if appropriate are the compression rates correct (eg have images been saved as TIFF files and/or JPEGs/GIFs at the appropriate compression ratio)?
3   Image quality
   • Have the correct bit-depths and resolutions been used?
   • Are the tonal values and colour balances correct?
   • Are the brightness and contrast settings correct?
   • Is the image as sharp and as clear as you required (for detail and edge detection)?
   • Is there any noticeable interference or noise?
   • Are there any notable missing lines or pixels (known as image artifacts)?
   • Have all the significant details noted in the assessment stages been successfully reproduced?

4   Output
- Have the images been checked on a variety of monitors?
- If print output is required, have the images been output to a variety of printers and the resulting quality checked (eg printed on a laser printer and a dye-sublimation machine if required)?

TASI, the UK's Technical Advisory Service for Images, has produced an excellent overview of QA entitled *Image quality and colour management issues* (**http://www.TASi.ac.uk/building/qa1.html**). In addition, a real-life example relating to the JIDI project is also presented (**http://www.TASi.ac.uk/building/jidiqa.html**).

Creating derivatives

A *derivative* can be defined as any object (analog or digital) derived from the *master* digital image produced in the scanning process. Thus a project may digitize at an extremely high level of quality (eg 24-bit colour, 600 dpi) and save these as their master images (usually as TIFF format). However, these files will be extremely large and unsuitable for quick distribution or dissemination via the Internet, and would not be suitable for browsable catalogues which only require thumbnails or low-resolution images. In this case, then, one would create a derivative from the TIFF image to something suitable for the end-purpose – eg convert the master image to JPEGs or GIFs, which will be much smaller in terms of file size.

Of course, image files can be handled at an individual level; this would require opening up each image, setting the requirements and output specifications, and then creating the derivative. Software packages such as Adobe Photoshop are extremely good at this fine-tuning of the image. Additionally, recent versions of Photoshop and many other image-handling packages (eg DeBabilzer Pro, ImageMagik, MrSid etc) will allow for *batch conversion* of images. Here the master images can be stored in a single folder or directory structure and then the software can be set to open and create the required derivative from each automatically. This could be done in theory without any further intervention by operators, leaving them to work on some other aspect of the project. Batch processing will also allow you to insert extra information into the image (such as watermarks or copyright notices). It should be noted, however, that the derivative may not always be digital. It could be a print copy to film (eg the computer output microfilm approach) or to high-quality paper, depending upon the aims of the original project or the preliminary user request.

The completed workflow

We are now in a position to bring all this information together concerning preparation, benchmarking, digitization and quality assurance checks into our expanded workflow. Looking back to Chapter 3, we can see that so far the digital imaging project has reached and completed the assessment stage. The proposed object or collection has been analysed in terms of how well it matches the needs of the institution, and how well it will satisfy the goals of increased access and preservation. In addition an initial digitization assessment has taken place to ascertain the probable method of digitization, and overall the project has been rated according to how feasible it will be to complete.

In this chapter the discussion has moved to the practical issue of the actual digitization and the steps involved. We have noted that, prior to the capture stage, the material has to be checked and prepared, and then sample shots taken to allow for accurate benchmarking. With this information the cameras can then be calibrated accordingly and digitization will be underway. At various stages throughout the actual conversion, however, quality assurance checks will have to be undertaken to ensure that the digital files being created match all expectations, including any derivatives that have been produced.

Graphically, this workflow could be represented as shown in Figure 4.1. The right-hand path reflects the course undertaken if the material is outsourced, whilst the left-hand side refers to in-house conversion.

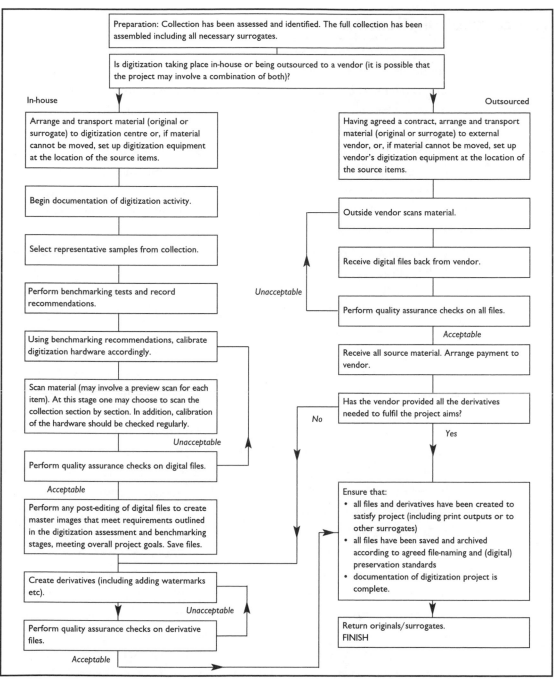

Fig. 4.1   *The completed workflow*

The costs of digitization

When we talk of the costs of digitization, we need to be exactly clear as to the boundaries of our discussion. In terms of this study, the costs of digitization simply refer to the amount of money that will be needed solely to deliver a digital image of a specific object, or of every object in a collection. That is to say, it does not cover the cataloguing of those objects, archiving, delivery or overall project management. It is only the cost of creating the digital file (master or derivative). Having simplified the scenario to a certain degree, one must now state that the problems with costing only this level of digitization are numerous, stemming mainly from the number of variables that can come into play. Tanner and Lomax (1999) conclude their informative study by suggesting that these variables would include such things as the resolution chosen, the bit-depth used, and such less technical issues as handling and preparation.

Throughout this book we have stated that there are two normal ways for digitization to take place: in-house or outsourcing. Let us look at each of these now in terms of cost factors.

If digitization were to take place in-house, then one would need to fund the necessary hardware, software, staff, accommodation and so on. The unit cost of digitizing a single image will be the amount needed to scan the entire collection divided by the number of items – eg if a camera costs £10,000 to purchase and operate, and it is being employed to scan 1000 images (and nothing else), then one could say that the unit cost of digitizing each image was £10. Of course this is somewhat divorced from reality, as hardware costs will often be spread over several projects, but staff can only be employed to carry out one scan at a time, and therefore the principle applies.

When it comes to outsourcing the digitization (ie using an external vendor), the contract will usually be based on a forecasted unit cost per image, probably resulting in an estimated overall fee for the whole project. This has the virtue of removing much of the administrative burden from the project manager, who then does not have to buy equipment, maintain it, hire and monitor staff, and so on. Yet at the same time we already know that outsourcing requires accurate QA checks and may be unfeasible in some situations (notably where the material cannot be removed from its normal location). It is often the case, then, that projects will tend to use a combination of in-house scanning (usually when it comes to rare items) and outsourcing (non-rare items and surrogates).

Let us now consider the factors that will influence the costs and cause them to vary considerably:

1   The nature of the source item: the original format of the item will influence its conversion costs. Not only will this include such things as original size and format, but also the care that must be taken when handling the item. Thus a project that is digitizing non-rare A4 documents will find that the unit cost of digitizing each item is extremely low, whereas a project that is dealing with rare items will present higher costs as each item requires special attention.

2   Throughput: the first factor is naturally followed by the issue of throughput. A4 sheets of paper can be processed quickly by such machines as sheet-feeders, and thus will involve less staff time (the same might apply for microfilm scanning for example). A collection made up of non-uniform sizes would involve much more direct intervention by the photographer to change scan area settings, recalibrate the cameras and so on. In other words, the type and range of variances in the source material will directly affect the speed at which it can be scanned – the general rule being that the longer the job takes to complete, the more it will cost.

3   Preparation: the level of preparation required to get the material ready for digitization will also influence cost. This may include transport (getting the source items to the place of digitization), assembling the full collection (correcting any omissions, for example), disbinding items or removing staples, and so on. If external vendors are used, they may offer to undertake these tasks for the project, but this will increase their fees.

4   Technical requirements: as was noted in Chapter 3, there is a trade-off between the quality of the image and storage. Similarly, there is a trade-off between quality and cost. A higher-resolution image will cost more to create than a low-resolution image. This is because better quality usually, though not always, requires more expensive equipment, and often leads to a much slower throughput. Similarly, higher quality results in larger file sizes, which occupy more space in the delivery medium, so there will be a higher cost for the CDs or ZIP drives required to ship the images back to the project.

Given the number of variables, many commentators on digitization seem to almost resign themselves to the fact that it is impossible to predict costs realistically. Yet this is unacceptable. It would be folly to embark on a digitization project without having some idea of how much it will cost. Indeed, when external funding is being sought, some indication of the costs for conversion will have to be given. Is it accurate to suggest, however, that this problem can ever be tackled?

The simplest and most effective way to produce a realistic estimate is to use the figures presented by previous projects that have been involved in digitization. Collated together, these will present reasonable reflections of the true costs of converting each image over a range of formats and resolutions. In doing this, one will quickly discover that costs reported will vary considerably and that one should therefore attempt to establish an average cost or a cost range. Gould and Ebdon (1999), for example, noted that in their world-wide survey of libraries involved in digitization the cost of digitizing a single page (though this was not clearly defined) varied from $7.72 up to $15.00.

Once these figures have been established, possibly in the form of a reference table (as in the example below), they can be applied to the digitization project in question and used in assessing its feasibility (see Chapter 3). If this is part of a longer process of digital activity, it is suggested that such a table is continually maintained and developed. To do this, however, there must be accurate knowledge of the collection itself. Experience has shown that curators of a collection are quite often unable to state the exact number of items and accurately list their conditions and formats; yet as noted above, all three are essential if one is being asked to cost a digital imaging project. A typical scenario all too often is one in which the curator points to a set of storage boxes saying 'that is the collection' without any specific information of what each box contains (beyond a standard finding aid).

However, assuming that one is in possession of accurate information about each item, and can state the technical requirements for the project in terms of resolutions, bit-depths, file formats, and so on then an estimate for the costs of digitization can be offered. In Tanner and Lomax (1999) a table of potential cost factors was presented which would indicate whether an item would fall into a low rating for digitization (£0.10–£0.20 per image), a medium rating

(£0.20–£1.50 per image), or a high rating (£1.50 and upwards). One should note here that the authors have placed great emphasis on the fact that costs for digitizing the same type of item can differ greatly from collection to collection. Using this method, the price matrix in Table 4.1 is presented as a guideline for the potential unit costs of digitizing. Along the top are the categories (and equally important the technical specifications) proposed by Tanner and Lomax. Their costs have therefore been aggregated with those presented by such projects as the University of Birmingham's BUILDER initiative, the JISC Image Digitization Initiative, the Internet Library for Early Journals and major studies in this area such as Kenney and Rieger (1998).

Table 4.1   *Unit costs per item averaged from various projects and reports*

	Printed A4 B&W	Bound A4 Volumes B&W	Printed A4 Paper (colour)	35-mm Microfilm B&W	Photographs 5"x4", and less than A3 manuscripts	35-mm Slides (colour)	Negative Photofilm unmounted	Glass Plates 5" × 4"
Suggested Digitization	300 dpi 1-bit B&W	400dpi 1-bit B&W	300dpi 8-bit Colour	400dpi 8-bit Greyscale	600dpi 24-bit Colour	2700dpi 24-bit Colour	2700dpi 8-bit Greyscale	600dpi 8-bit Greyscale
Average unit cost per item	£0.12 / $0.18	£0.60 / $0.88	£0.90 / $1.31	£0.50 / $0.73	£3.30 / $4.82	£2.20 / $3.21	£1.60 / $2.34	£11.20 / $16.36

We must again stress exactly what these costs are referring to, and what is not included in the estimate. The unit cost of digitization simply covers the amount of money needed to convert a single item of that format, at that resolution and bit-depth, to a digital file – and nothing more than that. As Steven Puglia (1999) observed, completed digital projects have noted that, of the amount of money they finally spent on the whole initiative only around a third (32%) went towards the digital conversion, with the remaining money going towards cataloguing and indexing (29%) and other activities such as management, administration, quality assurance and so on (39%). Real-life examples of this are widespread. For example the large US-based Making of America project (see Kenney and Rieger, 1998, 6) noted that 7% of costs went towards preparation, 50% to scanning, 36% to indexing and 7% to QA. In the UK the Internet Library of Early Journals (ILEJ) project, run by various UK universities, noted in its final report that each page cost c 18p to scan, but that on top of this each image cost 29p to index and

25p to process, bringing the true cost up to 75p per image (Leggate, 1997). The real cost of completing a digitization project, therefore, goes far beyond the unit cost of conversion. These are issues which will be explained further in Chapter 5.

A ready reckoner

It is clear from the above discussions that the problems of costing a projected digitization initiative are considerable. Variations in the formats and condition of the course material, not to mention the conversion techniques themselves, are coupled with major strategic decisions as to whether the conversion will take place in-house or be outsourced. In addition, although Table 4.1 gives a rough estimate of the unit cost of digitization, we have seen that these are aggregate prices, and the presence of aggregation implies that there is no clear-cut figure that one can quote. To make matters worse, digitization projects that have been completed indicate that the cost of conversion can prove to be as little as a third of the overall expenditure.

Faced with all these problems, it is tempting to say that no digitization project can be accurately costed beforehand. However, as we have noted above, funding bodies and senior managers will demand that estimated costings be presented when project proposals are submitted. How can the unfortunate staff member, placed in the position of completing such a bid, possibly hope to progress?

To assist such a person the following 'ready reckoner' is offered. Yet it is done so with several caveats in mind. The figures used are estimates, and all the variables noted above could mean that these prove to be too expensive, or in the worst case scenario far too cheap. To cater for the latter it is suggested that institutions new to digital imaging should build in contingency funds of at least 20%. Most importantly, this reckoner only goes as far as the digitization process, and does not include cataloguing and access (to be dealt with in Chapter 5). The example of ILEJ and Puglia's study suggest, therefore, that if one were to cost the delivery and archiving of a project, the figure presented by this reckoner should be doubled, or in some cases trebled. It is recommended, then, that this form is taken only as a starting point to be developed in the light of subsequent experiences; but at least it presents a base from which to work. A more elaborate exercise has been produced by the RLG entitled a *Worksheet for estimating digital reformatting costs*, using the material in Kenney and Rieger (1998). This should be consulted also as it provides a more developed discussion of the processes.

A digitization ready reckoner for time and cost

The following will provide you with a quick checklist to get some idea as to how much your digitization project will cost for the complete 'digital' capture of your archive. Note that this checklist does not cover factors such as marking up your material, or the final delivery of the archive for user access. The figures presented are based on aggregated figures from various projects and reports. In addition, this has taken into account the estimates provided in Kenney and Rieger (1998).

Preparation, selection, repair
Once the collection has been assessed and approved for digitization, the exact items will have to be selected and prepared. The following covers the time and cost for all these items, particularly those that need special attention. It should be noted, however, that many items in a collection can be selected and prepared in one stage if they are of reliable stock.

Books/serials
No of items   × 3 hrs   =   hr (a)

Folders (containing c.20 items)
No of folders   × 10 min   =   /60   =   hr (b)

Individual Items (single sheets, photographs, 35mm slides, etc.)
No of items   × 10 min   =   /60   =   hr (c)

     Total time to prepare material: a + b + c   =   hr (T1)

Total cost (assumes payment by hour for archivist, subject-specialist or project manager)

     No of hours (T1)   × £25.00/$30.00 =   £/$ (C1)

Additional costs for buying in items from other external collections, creating surrogates and transporting (+ insurance) of material to digitization centre.

No of items   × £/$ =   £/$ (C2)

Copyright

There are two costs involved in copyright. The first substantial cost, often overlooked, is the time involved in clearing copyright. The second is the payment to the copyright holders themselves for the right to use the material.

Time and financial costs are *per item*. An *item* here is any document or collection of documents covered by a single copyright. The timing of 5 hr takes into account finding the copyright holder and subsequent correspondences. To experienced people this may seem relatively short!

Time

No of items   × 5 hr   =   hr (T2)

Cost

Costs will vary considerably from request to request. Experience has shown that charges are usually either a one-off sum or per item.

No of items	×	£/$	per item = £/$
No of items	×	£/$	per item = £/$
No of items	×	£/$	per item = £/$

Total: £/$ (d)

and/or

Flat-fee payment of £/$
Flat-fee payment of £/$
Flat-fee payment of £/$

Total: £/$ (e)

Total costs d + e =   £/$ (C3)

Essential staffing costs

Here one costs for the members of staff working on the project, eg a manager, two

research officers, etc. Costs are calculated using the simple formula Number of staff ×
annual salary × length of project. **NB** for annual salary include full costs, ie national
insurance, pension etc.

Staffing level 1

| No of staff | × £/$ | pa × | years | = £/$ | (f) |

Staffing Level 2

| No of staff | × £/$ | pa × | years | = £/$ | (g) |

Management

| Hours per week | × | weeks (for | = | × £20.00/ ph = £/$ | (h) |
| | | full project) | | $29.50 | |

Consultancy

| Hours | × £/$ | ph = £/$ | | | (i) |

Overheads

This cost is not essential, but is often requested by administrators. It is calculated at a
usual rate of 45% of staff costs.

Overheads = f + g + h + i = £/$ × 45% = £/$ (overheads)

Total costs = f + g + h + i (+ 'overheads' optional) =   (C4)

Essential hardware costs

Assume 1 medium-level PC per person plus s/ware = c £1500/$2200

| No of computers | × | £1500/$2200 | = £/$ | (C5) |

Digitization

The costs and timings below are based on the experiences of various projects. These
figures target an average digitization project. There are many variables which may
influence these figures (more often than not by increasing the costs) such as the nature
of the primary source material and the sophistication of the hardware. Once again, these
are, of course, *aggregates* (ie the throughput for an eight-bit greyscale item is less than a
one-bit bi-tonal image). More elaborate figures, which tackle these variables, and also give
costs for a greater range of image quality, can be found in Kenney and Rieger (1998).

Benchmarking (involves digitizing a random sample of documents in order to find the
best settings).

No of sample documents   × 1 hr   =   hr (j)

In-house (cost here involves staff time, hardware and software)
Low-level scanning (A4 bi-tonal one-bit or greyscale eight-bit, c 100 per hour)
No of items   /100   =   hr (k)

Medium-level scanning (eg A4 300 dpi eight-bit colour, 35-mm slides and microfilm, c 50 per hour)
No of items   /50   =   hr (l)

High-level scanning (eg A3 or less 300–600 dpi 24-bit colour, c 20 per hour)
No. of items   /20   =   hr (m)

OCR Text (A4 document, scanning single sheet at a time)
No of items   /25   =   hr (n)

NB The figures above are very rough estimates using standard scenarios. Throughput will be reduced if documents are valuable, of different sizes etc. Conversely, high-end scanners which are digitizing similar-sized loose-leaf documents, can process c 350 items per hour. Again, for more accurate figures see Kenney and Rieger (1998).

Total time needed for in-house scanning j + k + l + m + n   =   hr (T3)

Research indicates that each full-time scanning technician will be able to devote c 1000 hours per annum to digitization.

No of full-time staff   × 1000 hrs =   hr (o)
available for scanning

Additional staff needed $\dfrac{(T3) - (o) =}{1000}$ (p)
for in-house scanning =

Additional costs required
for in-house scanning
No of staff   (p)   × £/$ pa   = £/$ (q)
or
No of extra hours   × £10.00/$15.00 ph   = £/$ (r)

Hardware/software
Flat-fee payment to cover *hardware* and *software* for scanning and digitization

(eg scanners and digitization software, extra PCs, storage etc) = £/$ (s)

Total cost for in-house scanning q + r + s   = £/$ (C6)

Outsource (includes costs for medium, shipping, master copies)
Low-level scanning
No of items   × 50p/$0.75   = £/$ (t)

Medium-level scanning
No of items   × £2.00/$3.00   = £/$ (u)

High-level scanning
No of items   × £10.00/$15.00 = £/$ (v)

Keying in
No of characters/1000   =   × £1.50/$2.20   = £/$ (wi)

OCR (explained in Chapter 5, here priced at 99.999% accuracy rate, but the cost would drop to £1.50/£   per page at a 98.5% accuracy rate)

No of pages   × £2.50/$3.65   = £/$ (wii)

Audio/video capture
No of clips, maximum 3 minutes each   × £5.00/$7.30 = £/$ (x)

          Total costs for outsourcing t + u + v + wi + wii + x = £/$ (C7)

Quality assurance
QA checks will need to be performed on the material returned. Generally, the full return is not checked but rather projects adopt a sampling approach (usually c 10%).

Total number of items in collection   /10 =   (y)
Based on 30 minutes to check each item
          _____ (y) / 2 =   (z) number of hours needed to perform QA
Total QA Costs (assumes payment by hour for archivist, subject-specialist or digitization expert)
          _____ (z) × £25.00/$31.50 = £/$ (C8)

Total costs for project C1 + C2 + C3 + C4 + C5 + C6 + C7 + C8

          = £/$

NB It is recommended that a contingency amount be built into the final total to cover unexpected additional costs. This could be as high as 20% if this is the first project initiated by the institution.

This checklist will give you a very rough estimate of the time and costs up to the point of assembling the digital archive (not creating the derivatives or saving/delivering the material). From here you will need to consider the creation of metadata, archiving and user access to the collection.

Importantly, this checklist spells out the costs in a very clinical fashion. When weighing up the pros and cons of digitizing in-house or outsourcing, one must consider the added value of having staff and expertise to hand for future projects, and the advantages of retaining staff and the manager's responsibility to make efforts to do so.

Chapter summary

In this chapter we have covered:

- preparation of material for digitization
- in-house and outsourcing
- the digitization workflow
- benchmarking and quality assurance checks
- what is meant by a derivative
- the costs of conversion
- a ready reckoner for costs.

5 | What else is needed? Cataloguing, delivery and completion

Introduction

Having now dealt with the digitization process in Chapter 4, some readers may be misled into thinking that the project has finally been completed. However, such an assumption would clearly be incorrect, and ignores many of the clues left at the end of the previous section. In the workflow covering the actual conversion process, it was noted that digitizers should attempt to document their work, and that once the digitization has taken place, they should deliver the item to the end-user. Documentation or cataloguing, and the eventual delivery of the digital collection, are just two issues that need to be addressed in this chapter. In addition, we need to discuss one derivative that is often overlooked in the literature, but in reality is very common in imaging projects, namely machine-readable text and optical character recognition (OCR). Furthermore, the issues of protecting images, copyright and watermarking also need analysis. Only then can we present a complete overview of the life-cycle of a digital imaging project.

Cataloguing and metadata

It will come as no surprise to curators or librarians to discover that cataloguing is one of the most crucial aspects of any digital imaging project. Puglia (1999) noted that cataloguing and indexing can account for nearly a third of the overall cost of the project. Without a browsable or searchable catalogue, end-users will struggle to find items in the collection they are seeking, the administrative team will have difficulties keeping track of the progress of the project (or any sales of the images), and digitizers will have lost an invaluable opportunity to record technical information that could prove essential in the future. Descriptive information attached to the digital object is commonly termed *metadata*. Simply put, metadata is data about data, or descriptive material that records a range of information about the digital object itself. This will be discussed at length later on in this chapter, but for now it raises an important question.

How does one catalogue digital images? There are two answers to this: one will seem very familiar to anyone involved in any previous cataloguing, whilst the second will probably be a new concept. To answer this question, then, one can catalogue digital images either using a standard text-based approach, or using *content-based image retrieval* (termed CBIR). A combination of the two approaches is also a possibility.

The text-based approach is by the far the most common system adopted by digitization projects. In this, one defines a catalogue structure of varying levels, and a structure for describing each individual object in the collection. If you are cataloguing a digital facsimile of a painting, for example, your structure may include fields to hold the name of the artist, the accepted title of the picture, its date of composition and so on. This is the type of activity that has been developed and practised in libraries, museums and galleries for many centuries. The advantages of this approach are:

- it allows for highly structured text records to be created containing as much or as little information as required
- it is familiar to cataloguers and users
- it is a proven system in both the analog and digital world.

There are, however, some disadvantages to this approach. First, cataloguers can often find it difficult to be objective in their descriptions, and have to be trained to use an accepted way of recording information (eg using a thesaurus of accepted keywords). Consequently, the way the user can access the collection is dictated by the catalogue itself. Most importantly, though, it can be an extremely labour-intensive process (not to mention tedious).

This has led many people to look at a means of automatically extracting information from the image which can then be indexed and searched. This is known as content-based image retrieval (CBIR). In essence, CBIR software, which uses advanced algorithms, can process an image by extracting information about the colours used, the textures and the various shapes in the picture. For example, CBIR software, when faced with a picture of the Union Jack, could automatically extract information about the colours (red, white and blue) and the shapes and patterns within the flag. This information could be stored in an index which the user could then search to look for all images that contain a Union Jack (by formulating a query based on the colours, the pattern or both). Such a system offers the project the advantages of speed when compared to manual cataloguing, objectivity, a range of different ways of searching for the image, and of course it is automatic. At present, however, CBIR software is extremely limited, allowing only simple queries to be formulated. This is due entirely to the fact that only basic information (generated by the algorithm) is actually being recorded. It cannot, for example, automatically determine authorship, titles and provenance, and one questions how many users would be satisfied with its results. It is also an unfamiliar process to many 'traditional' users, who are accustomed to searching catalogues by lemmatization, not shapes – so much so that evaluations have shown that it requires a lot more browsing on the part of users before they can begin to get meaningful results. Furthermore, it can be very inaccurate. Although in the above example the software may find images of the Union Jack, it may also retrieve any images that have a large quantity of the three colours or a series of crosses and triangles. As the aim of most digitization projects is to achieve the widest possible access to the images, but at the same time maintain a degree of relevancy and accuracy, it is not surprising to find that nearly all imaging projects (commercial and public-sector) adopt the text-based approach to cataloguing. This may, however, change in the future as CBIR software increases in accuracy and sophistication; industry can certainly see strong advantages in an effective and powerful system for the automatic content indexing of images.

Text-based cataloguing and metadata

Text-based cataloguing provides the most straightforward approach to recording information about the digital collection. In order to implement this, the project will have to decide on the structure of its catalogues and the resulting format – in other words, one will need to establish an appropriate metadata system. There is a tendency to delay the decision as to which metadata system one employs until a decision has been reached on the delivery system to be used by the project. However, this is unwise and is a clear case of the tail wagging the dog. The metadata system that is chosen should be designed to meet the current and future requirements of the project and its users. This should not be compromised simply because of limitations in a database or indexing system.

Metadata as a term has crept into the standard vocabulary of IT-related projects in the last few years and has often led to much confusion. However, the concept behind metadata is hardly new as we are used to providing metadata for printed material, eg in the form of the imprint page and the library catalogue. This information serves to record a set of standard information for administrative records, for citing the source, and of course to help to find it in the first place. Metadata in the IT world serves similar purposes. Sometimes it will record information about the creator and project, sometimes it will provide information describing the contents of the object so that users will be helped in locating it, and more often than not it provides a mixture of both of these and more.

The Colorado Digitization Project (**http://coloradodigital.coalliance. org/question.html**) states that for metadata one should begin by asking:

- what metadata scheme are you planning to use
- what type of description already exists for the collection, and at what level (item level, collection level etc)
- where there are several versions of an original, which version you will catalogue.

The inherent problems with metadata when it comes to digital imaging are:

1 There is no single accepted standard for cataloguing all material in electronic form.
2 Existing print-based catalogues for collections are often incomplete.
3 Metadata systems can quickly grow into something that is too large to be realistically instigated.

4   Metadata systems often lose sight of user requirements.

However, to a certain degree most metadata will almost write itself. It is fairly standard to include something such as:

- author or creator
- publication/creation date
- a title
- a summary
- project details.

Beware of the fact that this list can soon grow into dozens of categories of information, many of which cannot be described on account of time constraints. Similarly, it is often the case that the information is simply not available and for many items the majority of categories would remain empty. Arms (1996) notes that:

> To prepare individual full catalogue records for all the items in the collections that the Library plans to digitize would not only be futile in many cases . . . it would be totally infeasible. At UC Berkeley, it was estimated that it would take the entire cataloguing staff from all Berkeley libraries 400 years to catalogue the collection of 3.5 million images. Use must be made of descriptions that already exist. The practices of archival communities that are less expensive than item–level cataloguing must be integrated into automated systems.

This raises some important issues – namely that the time involved in implementing and maintaining a metadata system is considerable, and that the presence of existing metadata (be it hand–written on cards, printed or electronic) will have important implications for the feasibility of the project. When a collection is being assessed for digitizing, one of the points we noted earlier for consideration was whether sufficient cataloguing of the collection was already available. In particular could this be transposed into an electronic catalogue, allowing unique identification of the individual digital object. If not, the costs for cataloguing will have to be included, as the success of a large digital collection rests on the user's ability to find individual items.

Successful metadata

In the full digital imaging project, metadata will be created by a variety of people, and in turn will be used by various parties. In brief, the successful metadata system should satisfy the needs of the following:

- cataloguers
- users
- technical experts
- administrators.

To achieve this it will need to contain information created by most of the people listed above, and usable by all. It should allow cataloguers to record all the information they wish to about the digital images. It should allow users multiple access points to the collection so that they can find particular objects through a variety of searches. The technical experts will want information on the digital file itself to help with such things as future benchmarking, migration and preservation; and the administrator may want the metadata to help with e-commerce facilities. To elaborate, then, the interested parties and their concerns can be summarized as:

- cataloguers, who will need full flexibility to enter all the information they wish to about a particular item, and with the ease with which traditional cataloguing is performed
- users, who will want the facilities to browse and search for items, to locate freely available digital surrogates quickly, and possibly to order/request restricted-access surrogates
- technical experts, who will need a system that allows full information to be entered about the digitization process and subsequent derivatives, and data that will aid future preservation of the material
- administrators, who will require readily accessible information about the

'life' of the digital object, its provenance, its management and its subsequent distribution, and the ability to identify an object quickly in order to speed up its delivery to the end-user (with respect to meeting orders).

To outline some general rules of thumb, the metadata system one should be striving for must:

- be flexible, extensible and forward-looking
- allow for easy input by the various cataloguers (ie it should not be an 'overkill' solution requiring the recording of irrelevant information, or data which is simply not available)
- allow for easy searching and browsing by the user, but with the functionality to allow it to deal with highly complicated searches
- be able to deal with all kinds of digital objects from all manner of collections
- be accessible outside the institution and possibly as part of existing online catalogues (such as a library's OPAC)
- allow for different points of access to the collections – ie it should be able to handle items (such as a book) and individual objects (eg texts or images within the book) and have means of describing and discriminating between both.

Which metadata system?

In a sense this is the wrong question to ask. More correctly, one should begin by asking what exactly one wishes to record about the individual item and how that will be used by the project and its end-users. We have outlined the possible requirements of the interested parties above but these need to be explored a bit more.

Let us consider an archive of photographs. What would one expect to see in a catalogue describing the objects in the collection? Some general categories immediately spring to mind such as date, photographer, provenance, content, condition, shelfmark or collection number, size, colour information and so on. If all of these were listed in some catalogue or finding aid (electronic or not), then the end-user would stand a fairly good chance of finding a photograph relating to their interests. If we were to digitize the photographs, we might then want to insert additional metadata (or cataloguing information) such as date of creation, file format (eg TIFF, JPEG, GIF), resolution, bit-depth, file size, file dimensions and so on. This of course can be extended, as a digital imaging project may wish to record the following (note the inclusion of post-processing techniques such as highlighting):

- name or number (unique identifier for digital file)
- date created
- creator
- mode (eg bi-tonal, greyscale)
- resolution
- file type
- highlight
- shadow
- gamma setting
- height
- width
- size (Mb)
- original
- contrast applied (curves, levels, brightness, contrast)
- scanner
- compression.

The list is extensive, and one of the truths about metadata is that it can quite quickly get out of hand. The problem for the digital imaging project, once it has identified all the categories it wishes to use to describe and monitor a digital file, is to find a system that can cope with such complexities.

Yet it is clear from the above that, when complex metadata is being created, the limitations of these and other more traditional library cataloguing systems (such as MARC), will quite quickly be exposed. Indeed, even more recent systems developed specifically with the electronic environment in mind – such as Dublin Core and the Resource Description Framework (RDF) – can also be outstripped by such requirements. Therefore many large digital imaging projects have looked elsewhere for an underlying system that is both flexible enough to cope with the complexities we have noted, and at the same time easy to use and implement. The solution that has most widely been adopted is that of the Standard Generalized Mark-up Language (SGML), or increasingly its most recent descendent, the Extensible Mark-up Language (XML). It is also possible to combine more than one of these systems. For example, the RDF could be used as the means of cataloguing for the web (the public face of the collection) but built-in references could link to more extensively marked-up documents using SGML/XML. This is a commonly adopted policy, and seems to be logical and practical.

Previous studies

Before proceeding to a discussion of SGML/XML, it is worth noting some of the previous or ongoing projects and studies which surround the area of metadata. The CURL Exemplars for Digital Archives (CEDARS) project (**http://www.curl.ac.uk/cedarsinfo.shtml**) is worthy of mention, but primarily from the stance of preserving the digital object. The findings of CEDARS will be extremely influential on any future digital initiatives and will undoubtedly be taken on board by future digital imaging projects (be they commercial or otherwise). As part of its working brief, CEDARS has commissioned an extensive study of the various metadata standards available (Day, 1998). In the study, Day provides brief descriptions of many of the major metadata systems, links to further documentation, and a discussion of the issues that each one attempts to tackle and their methodology (including a list of the entities/fields which each records data under).

Like many other projects, CEDARS has recognized the need for a comprehensive metadata system that caters for all the needs outlined above, and is currently looking at the Open Archival Information System. This system, originating from the space industry, sets out to define a conceptual model for archiving digital data that recognizes the need to cater for receiving the digital object, distributing the digital object and archiving the digital object (by defining different 'information packages' for each stage). It is also in keeping with the findings of other national projects on digital preservation and metadata (such as Australia's PANDORA projects and the Netherlands' NEDLIB initiative).

Elsewhere, at the beginning of its funding, the JIDI (JISC Image Digitization Initiative) project set out a lengthy set of definitions for metadata categories to deal with image collections. Its approach was to segment the cataloguing into five levels: the *collection*, the *work*, the *visual document*, the *person*, and the *organization*. The project then defined these levels and suggested the types of descriptive elements that could be identified under each:

Collection

An aggregate of one or more works or visual documents (see below). This idea would be extremely useful at the level of such things as a manuscript, where individual visual documents represent folios or pages. Containing:

- title
- description
- size
- owner
- copyright owner
- copyright statement
- copyright status
- notes.

Work

The physical object that has existed at some time in the past, or an ephemeral event (performance) that has been captured in physical form. Containing:

- ID
- title
- description
- subject
- X-dimension
- Y-dimension
- dimension units

- type
- material
- technique
- creator
- date
- repository name
- original site
- provenance
- copyright owner
- style/period
- nationality/culture
- related work
- relationships
- notes.

Visual document

An image that depicts a work (be it photographic or digital). Containing:

- document ID
- type
- format
- date
- owner
- description
- subject
- origin
- copyright owner
- copyright status
- relationships
- source
- X-dimension
- Y-dimension
- dimension units.

For digital files only:

- file name
- scan resolution
- bit-depth
- file size
- colour space
- compression type
- compression ratio
- capture device
- creator
- notes.

Person

Recording information about an individual. Containing:

- ID
- title
- forenames
- surname
- alternative names
- date of birth
- date of death
- address
- e-mail
- phone
- notes.

Organization

Containing:

- ID

- name
- other name
- address
- e-mail
- phone
- notes.

To conclude this briefest of surveys into other studies it is worth noting the RLG's Working Group on the Preservation Issues in Metadata. The Report's (1998) findings recommended 16 categories under which a digital master image should be recorded:

- date
- transcriber (name of person responsible for transcribing the metadata)
- producer
- capture device
- capture details
- change history
- validation key (a verification system)
- encryption
- watermark
- resolution
- compression
- source
- colour
- colour management
- colour bar/greyscale
- control targets.

There are, of course, many other studies into cataloguing and metadata systems, some of which are listed in Appendix C. However, we can abstract an important point from the above. The description elements that CEDARS, JIDI and the RLG identified are extensive, complex and overlapping. To reiterate, if the findings of these elements are typical of those that a digital imaging project will face, then one clearly needs to identify a flexible metadata system that can accommodate such requirements. To return to the point made earlier, the SGML/XML approach seems to offer the best possible solution for this at the moment.

SGML, HTML, and XML

SGML is an acronym for the Standard Generalized Mark-up Language, registered as an international industry standard. It provides a way of defining how one marks up documents, or in this case the catalogues for digital imaging projects. It is not owned by any single commercial company, and does not provide a single mark-up scheme for one to follow (though there are plenty of 'flavours' of SGML around). There are numerous advantages to using SGML and these are well documented in other publications. However, it would not be amiss to list some of the most important ones here:

1   SGML is an international industry standard.
2   SGML is non-proprietary and thus platform and software-independent.
3   SGML uses only standard ASCII characters and is thus easily transferable from software to software and across networks.
4   The use of ASCII, and a zero reliance on proprietary software, ensures longevity for documents marked up in SGML.
5   SGML allows for highly sophisticated levels of mark-up.
6   SGML documents can easily convert to other formats (eg HTML, LaTeX), thus making it a good 'base' providing one-to-many functionality (very similar then to the master image approach identified earlier).

The most widespread occurrence of SGML is the web itself, using a 'flavour' of SGML known as HTML (the HyperText Mark-up Language). Simply put, SGML tells you how you can define the way you mark up your documents, and HTML is an application of this. Thus all HTML (if it is valid) is SGML, but not all documents which claim to use SGML are HTML.

This situation can be explained by the document type definition or DTD. This is akin to a set of rules in which you define the type of mark-up you will be using, what it can contain, where it can occur and so on. All SGML documents require a DTD so that you can check that the document is valid (ie obeys all the rules set out in the DTD) and understand what all the mark-up is meant to indicate.

What does this imply for the digital imaging project? In short, if one accepts that SGML is the best way to provide a flexible metadata system that can deliver both complexity and ease of use (plus longevity), then one could be tempted to use HTML (a flavour of SGML after all) to create the catalogues needed. Indeed, many digital imaging projects have done just that – mounting 'catalogues' (which in effect are simply HTML lists) on the web. To understand why this is not recommended, and why one should invest the time and money into exploring more complicated DTDs in SGML or XML, one needs to discuss the limitations of HTML.

HTML is extremely good for what it sets out to do: publish material on the web. It allows you to tell a browser to display a piece of text in bold, or italic, or blue – in other words, all of the tags are aimed at displaying the text in a certain manner. Furthermore, HTML is very free and easy with its mark-up. For example, the HTML DTD does not prohibit one from putting a <H1> tag after a <H3>. On the face of it this may seem a good thing but many cataloguers would probably state that this means it is not very formal about the structure of documents. Moreover, let us suppose that one was not interested in marking up pieces of text as bold or italic, but instead wished to indicate their role or place in the structure (eg the catalogue for the digital imaging project would want strict fields for inserting data to be recorded and understood by the subsequent delivery system). HTML in its present form does not provide any tags for performing more non-format-oriented mark-up. One solution could be to try to extend the HTML DTD to bring in new tags, but then one is immediately creating problems by moving away from what most normal web browsers expect and are equipped to take, with non-standard tags. Therefore the other solution (and the one recommended here) is to abandon HTML as the mark-up used for cataloguing and to search around to look for other DTDs which allow for more complicated mark-up and are more suited for cataloguing digital imaging projects.

Thankfully there are DTDs which match these requirements. However, before we consider two such DTDs, we need to explain the role of XML, the latest development in the SGML world. XML stands for the Extensible Mark-up Language and is designed to tackle the problems noted above – namely, to combine the popularity and ease of HTML (whilst recognizing its limitations) with the versatility and more organized approach of full SGML (but again overcoming many of the problems of implementing this). Led and promoted by the World Wide Web Consortium (W3C), XML is becoming the universal language for data on the web. Like SGML and HTML, XML is a set of tags and declarations – but rather than being concerned with formatting information on a page, XML focuses on providing information about the data itself (ie much more akin to SGML). As Brisson (1998) notes in his survey of cataloguing and digital libraries:

> XML can be categorized as an 'intelligent' HTML. The source of this characterization is the ability for XML, like SGML, to allow a website designer . . . to define the types of tags used in a website.

Apart from its closeness to SGML (at the same time it is much easier to use), XML is the language of e-commerce. It allows for easy identification and administration of digital objects, particularly on the Internet.

All these factors are increasingly making XML the metadata system of choice for digital imaging projects and digital libraries projects. The Harvard VIA (Visual Information Access) initiative (see Appendix A) has chosen XML as the metadata system behind its digital library collections, allowing users to search across five participating libraries utilizing its Z39.50 compliance – an information retrieval standard, or protocol, which allows for communication and searching across different catalogues (Braid, 1999). Similar initiatives using XML have been running successfully for some time at the Universities of Virginia and Michigan, and the Library of Congress.

More flavours of XML: the Text Encoding Initiative (TEI) and the Encoded Archival Description (EAD) DTDs

Assuming that one accepts that XML is the metadata system of choice, the next step is to consider which flavour of XML to use. By *flavour*, it is perhaps more precise to refer to the types of tags and attributes allowed by the chosen brand of XML. In XML, as in SGML, these are dictated by the DTD. Leaving aside the possibility of writing one's own DTD, most digital imaging projects select one that is already written – an off-the-shelf DTD that contains all the rules and definitions for the tags one can use. At present, there are two DTDs that are generally chosen by digitization projects: the Text Encoding Initiative and the Encoded Archival Description.

The Text Encoding Initiative (TEI) project was established in 1987 under the joint sponsorship of the Association for Computers and the Humanities, the Association for Computational Linguistics and the Association for Literary and Linguistic Computing. It was aimed at meeting the needs of textual scholars who required a set of highly sophisticated tag sets to mark up documents. In May 1994, the TEI issued its *Guidelines for the encoding and interchange of machine-readable texts* (Burnard and Sperberg-McQueen, 1994) which proposed hundreds of tags via a series of DTDs. In 1995, these were reviewed and a selection of the most used tags were collected together under a single DTD known as TEI-lite. Importantly for this book, these tags are being used by digital imaging projects as the base for their cataloguing system, as they allow you to enter data into fields covering many of the requirements noted above. Furthermore, because of its origins, the TEI will allow for meticulous description of textual documents (going right down to parts of speech). Figure 5.1 provides an example of an extract from the TEI header. Here one can clearly see the use of the tags to define specific bibliographic information that would be directly applicable to cataloguing the object. As any DTD can be extended, it is theoretically possible that if the TEI DTD does not have the tag needed to catalogue a particular item in a collection, one could re-edit the DTD and add this extra information. However, experience shows that this is not to be recommended unless one has considerable expertise to hand.

```
<TEIHEADER TYPE="TEXT" DATE.CREATED="1997-12-18">
      <FILEDESC>
      <TITLESTMT>Return of the Native A machine readable edition
             <AUTHOR>Hardy, Thomas</AUTHOR>
      </TITLESTMT>
      <EXTENT>
             <SEG TYPE="size">B</SEG>
             <SEG TYPE="format">unspecified</SEG>
             <SEG TYPE="location">offline</SEG>
      </EXTENT>
      <PUBLICATIONSTMT>
             <AUTHORITY ID="HARMI2">Deposited by Gutenberg, Project
                   <ADDRLINE>405 West Elm Street</ADDRLINE>
                   ...
                   <DATE>1994-03-20</DATE>
             </AUTHORITY>
             <DISTRIBUTOR>
                   <ADDRLINE>Oxford Text Archive </ADDRLINE>
                   ...
                   <ADDRLINE>http://ota.ahds.ac.uk</ADDRLINE>
             </DISTRIBUTOR>
             <IDNO TYPE="ota">hard2053</IDNO>
             <AVAILABILITY STATUS="FREE">Freely available for non-commercial use
             provided that this header is included in its entirety with any copy distributed
             </AVAILABILITY>
      <PUBLICATIONSTMT>
      <SOURCEDESC><BIBL><NOTE></NOTE></BIBL></SOURCEDESC>
      </FILEDESC>
      <ENCODINGDESC>
             <EDITORIALDECL>Editorial practices unknown</EDITORIALDECL>
             <REFSDECL>Reference system unknown</REFSDECL>
             <CLASSDECL>
                   <TAXONOMY ID=LCSH>
                         <BIBL>Library of Congress Subject Headings</BIBL>
                   </TAXONOMY>
                   ...
             </CLASSDECL>
      </ENCODINGDESC>
      <PROFILEDESC>
             <CREATION>
                   <DATE VALUE="?" CERTAINTY="CA"></DATE>
             </CREATION>
             <LANGUSAGE>
                   <LANGUAGE ID="eng" USAGE="100">English</LANGUAGE>
             </LANGUSAGE>
             <TEXTCLASS>
                   <KEYWORDS SCHEME="otash">
                   <TERM TYPE="genre">Unspecified</TERM>
                   </KEYWORDS>
                   ...
      </PROFILEDESC>
      <REVISIONDESC>
             <CHANGE>
                   <DATE>1997-12-18</DATE>
                   <RESPSTMT>Burnard, Lou<RESP> </RESP></RESPSTMT>
                   <ITEM>Header auto-generated from TOMES</ITEM>
             </CHANGE>
      </REVISIONDESC>
</TEIHEADER>
```

Fig. 5.1   *An example of using the TEI DTD to mark up bibliographic information about an item (in this case Hardy's* The Return of the Native)

Notes: The above is an extract from the TEI Header, which is mandatory. The use of '...' denotes an omission for the purposes of this example. This could be linked by using various tags or elements to digital images of the book (or pages within the book).

On account of the literary and linguistic background to the TEI (not to mention its possible complexity) many people have looked to other DTDs for their projects. The notable example of this is the EAD (Encoded Archival Description) DTD, which focuses on museum and archive collections. This grew out of the recognition that many collections had as a catalogue some form of finding aid of varying complexity. Taking this idea as a base, tags were designed and developed to reflect this level of cataloguing (which is often very cursory). Figure 5.2 contains an example of using the EAD.

The EAD then, once it was launched, seemed very attractive to curators and librarians as it emanated from a background of archival descriptions. It is very common, therefore, to see a digital imaging project declare that its metadata system is using XML based on the EAD DTD. It should be noted, however, that it is also possible to combine the EAD and TEI by using the EAD as the umbrella mark-up system for cataloguing at a general level and then bringing in the TEI for encoding the contents of individual items to a much more sophisticated level.

In summary, then, the adoption of XML seems increasingly to be the norm in digital imaging projects nowadays (though there are exceptions, of course, as we will see below). Following on from this, most digital imaging projects are choosing either the TEI flavour (DTD) of XML, the EAD DTD, or occasionally a combination of both.

Final considerations: describing content, file naming structures and creation of metadata

Let us now consider a typical example that often confronts people involved in text-based cataloguing of digital images. Let us suppose that three cataloguers were each given a photograph of a cricket match in progress and asked independently to describe the content of the image. When the returns are analysed it is found that the first simply described the content as being 'a sporting

```
<c01 langmaterial="Latin">
    <did>
        <unitid type="Shelfmark">MS. Don. e. 128</unitid>
        <unittitle>
            <persname role="Author">Jerome</persname>, <title>Letters</title>, Pt. I
            <geogname role="Place of origin">England</geogname>
            <unitdate>15th century, <emph render="italic">c</emph>. 1450-60(?)
            </unitdate>
        </unittitle>
        <physdesc>
            <genreform>Codex</genreform>
            <physfacet type="Material">Parchment.</physfacet>
            <dimensions type="Leaf" unit="mm">The leaves c.175 x
            120 mm.</dimensions>
            <extent>ii (paper) + I (original parchment) + 256 + I (original(?)
            parchment), + iii (paper).</extent>
            <physfacet type="Foliation">Foliated in modern pencil, i-iii,
            1-260.</physfacet>
            <physfacet type="Collation">In quires of eight leaves:...
            ...the first 25 quires only: '+', a-f, j-o, g-h, p-z, '[tironian] &amp;'.
            </physfacet>
            <physfacet type="Ruling">Frame ruled in brown crayon; the ruled
            space <emph render="italic">c</emph>.120 x 80 mm.</physfacet>
            <physfacet type="Script">Written by <persname role="Scribe">Robert
            Flemmyng</persname> (see under Provenance) in Italian humanistic scripts,
            with 20 or 21 lines per page.</physfacet>
            ...
        </physdesc>
    </did>
    <scopecontent>
        <head>Text</head>
        <list>
            <item>1. (fol. iii recto-verso) Numbered list of contents. </item>
            <item>2. (fols. 1-256) <persname role="Author">Jerome</persname>, Letters
            (nos. 1-47 in the collection of 123): '<emph render="italic">Epistola Damasi
            pape ad hieronimum presbiterum</emph> Dilecto in christo filio hieronimo...
            ...no. 35, etc.).
            </item>
        </list>
    </scopecontent>
    <scopecontent>
        <head>Decoration</head> <p>One four-line 'puzzle' ...
        ...subsequent letters.</p>
    </scopecontent>
    <admininfo>
        <custodhist> <head>Provenance</head><p>1. Copied, probably in England, in
        humanistic script by <persname role="Owner">Robert Flemmyng</persname>,...
        ...by the Bodleian through Sotheby's by private treaty, in memory of <persname>R.
        W. Hunt</persname>, and paid for with the help of donations from his friends,
        1980.</p>
        </custodhist>
    </admininfo>
    <add>
        <bibliography><head>Bibliography</head> <p> <bibref>'Notable accessions:
        western manuscripts', <title>Bodleian Library Record</title>, 10...
        ...on themes selected and described by some of his friends</title> (Oxford,
        Bodleian Library, 1980), no. XXI. 6, fig. 65 (fols. iii verso-1r).</bibref></p>
        </bibliography>
    </add>
</c01>
```

The catalogue entry is divided into several notable sections:

- identifying the object (including shelfmark, origin, etc)
- description of the physical object (including material, collation and so on)
- contents of the object (using a list scheme)
- extra information (such as provenance, related reading and so on).

Notes: The use of '...' implies a deliberate omission for the purposes of this example. Within the mark-up one could include <extptr> and <extref> (extended pointer and extended reference) tags or <altformavail> to point to digital images of the manu-script.

Fig. 5.2   *An example of cataloguing an item (in this case a manuscript) using the Encoded Archival Description DTD*

event' and left it at that; the second cataloguer elaborated slightly and recorded 'a game of cricket, showing fielders, bowlers and batsmen'; whereas the third cataloguer, obviously displaying a knowledge of the game produced 'a test match, cricket, England playing Australia, bowlers, batsmen, wicket keeper, umpire, fielders appealing for a catch'. Although this is an extreme example, it illustrates the problems one faces when attempting to describe the content of an image, especially if the cataloguing is being performed by a range of people. Left to their own devices, and without any supervision, cataloguers who are asked to describe an image will find it very difficult to be entirely objective, allowing their own perceptions and knowledge to creep in. This will cause considerable problems when it comes to using the catalogue. For example, in the above scenario of the cricket match, if end-users searched for images of 'sport/sport*' they would only find the photograph if it had been catalogued by the first person. Alternatively, if they were interested in any photographs depicting sporting events in which teams from Australia were participating, then only the third, more detailed entry would yield a result.

CBIR, noted above, would get around this problem as it is entirely objective. But, as has already been stated, its functions are extremely limited at the moment and therefore text-based cataloguing has to be employed. To overcome the problems of subjectivity, it is essential that the cataloguing (and not just of the content of the image) is supervised and controlled. This could be done by issuing a set vocabulary or thesaurus of terms which cataloguers have to use (with no digressions). Some large projects (such as CORBIS or the Getty Images) have established their own controlled vocabularies, but this is often not an option for smaller projects. In the case of the latter, as with the DTDs discussed above, it is best to adopt an already established (and publicly available) standard such as the Library of Congress thesaurus for graphic material, or the ICONCLASS system (especially suited for classical and fine art images). These will enforce on the cataloguer an exact set of keywords, terms and so on which they will have to use when describing the digital images, thus ensuring a degree of uniformity across the collection. Such keywords can be entered as plain text or numerical values into the appropriate field in the XML document.

This need for unambiguous cataloguing and consistency appears in another important area of creating metadata: namely the identifiers one gives to individual files. These object names or file names are the 'bare bones' metadata that always accompany the digital object. In that sense, then, if all other metadata were lost, the file name might be the only information one had about the content without actually opening the image (a cumbersome task). Therefore it is essential that the names given to files are:

- meaningful (conveying information about the file and its relation to other files)
- consistent
- persistent.

Taking these points in order, the first stresses the need to convey some form of meaning in the file name. The most obvious example (when digitizing images from books) would be using a file-naming system that reflects the shelfmark of the volume. For example, the filename 'ms22f1r.jpg' would suggest immediately that this is an image of folio one, recto, from manuscript number 22. Similarly, the .JPG suffix could indicate that this is a derivative of a master TIFF image (.TIF). Directory structures can assist in this, of course, but one should be wary of relying on these if the files are being moved around frequently on an individual and not a full collection basis.

There are no rules on how one names files, although many people would advise that the eight–three rule is still observed (ie eight characters followed by a three-character suffix for the file format, such as 'abcdefgh.tif'), or at the very least a fixed width or number of characters prior to any suffix. Furthermore, it is recommended that blank spaces and control characters in file identifiers should be avoided. Outside these, the only real rule is consistency. Choose the file-naming system beforehand and stick to it, unless subsequent events mean you have to reconsider the original decisions.

Users are frequently frustrated by the fluid state of web pages and their sudden disappearance, rendering URLs obsolete. It is therefore important that the identifiers one uses for the digital file are persistent – hence the notion of *persistent* URLs (PURLs). The most recent developments point towards the use of a digital object identifier (DOI) – a unique identifier for a file, combining the URL with a uniform resource name (URN), which is independent of the file's location. DOIs can seem somewhat confusing at first, and in smaller projects this may not concern the project managers, as their main concern is consistency, meaning and a degree of persistency. However, larger imaging projects that form part of an institutional commitment should look seriously at the recent developments in this area. Day (1999) also notes that legacy identifiers such as ISBN numbers could be employed to help identify a file, but these are often too lengthy for some systems.

Whichever choice is made, once the file-naming system has been decided upon it should be adhered to. If the digitization is being outsourced, then the file-naming must be included in the contract, and when the files are received back from the external agency, the QA checks must include looking at the identifiers particularly, as accurate file-name conversion using batch processes is not always straightforward.

Yet let us not be fooled by what has been proposed in the previous discussions and recommendations. The actual cataloguing of the items to be retrieved through searching or browsing – that is, the creation of the metadata itself – can and will involve a considerable amount of work. Although we have touched on this already, the point is worth reinforcing. The cataloguing work to be undertaken has to be planned for and costed if one is to deliver the digital images successfully. It is, of course, a difficult task to work out how much time (and hence money) one will need to catalogue a particular item or collection of items. Yet one can list obvious determining factors such as the decisions made in conjunction with the four key parties – cataloguers/curators, technical experts, administrators and representative users – as to what level of cataloguing is appropriate for the project. In general, though, it is advised that projects should not overload their cataloguing with superfluous or difficult-to-find categories. Some projects adopt the approach of cataloguing every item to a basic level which would satisfy the majority of users, and then returning later, time and money permitting, to add more detail. Others keep down costs by reusing existing catalogues (paper-based or electronic) wherever possible by attempting to generate some of the metadata automatically. The latter is most easily performed in terms of the technical metadata, and relies on the sophistication of the software used (usually at the capturing stage). Ideally this should automatically provide and save information about the file name, the file format, file dimensions, file size, capture details and other boiler-plate text, and automatically insert these into a database, thus removing the onus on the digitizer to update the record manually after each capture.

Apart from automatic creation, the other approach is actually to key in the information. In most digital imaging projects, the metadata will be built up over time – eg some initial administrative data will be entered, followed by technical information, and then (usually after conversion) the cataloguers will provide the content and bibliographic information. Again the important point is consistency. Several cataloguers may be working on different items from the same collection, but the manager of the project needs to know they are recording the metadata uniformly. If one adopts the SGML/XML approach, one also needs to ensure that the data being entered is appropriate and in keeping with the chosen DTD – it is valid (tools such as SoftQuad's Author/Editor, Xmetal or GNU's EMACS) as checking is done against the DTD throughout. To assist in all of this it is suggested that a uniform interface be designed for all the cataloguers (be they administrative, technical or bibliographic), clearly setting out the categories where the information is required, and which data should go where. This could then be collated automatically into one record for the digital object.

Delivery systems

Flat-file browsing

Having spent some time discussing the possible complexities of the metadata system, it may seem strange to begin this section on delivery systems by looking at simple flat-file browsing. However, it is important to explore this solution of delivering digital images to the end-user. In this scenario a single flat-file or a series of linked files is presented, more often than not as a straightforward list of all the items, some of which may have additional information. These descriptions are then simply linked to the digital image. An obvious example of this would be to mount a web page created in HTML which contains a single reference to each of the digital objects and use a simple hyperlink to bring up the image itself. In theory this could be searched by using the FIND command available in a standard web browser, or if the site consists of several pages, by using an index and search engine such as Glimpse. This is a quick-and-easy solution, and thus understandably attractive to many projects. However, it is also extremely unsophisticated from both the cataloguer's and the user's perspective. Complicated searches are not available, nor can one easily hide information (such as technical metadata) which is not necessarily of interest. Above all, the administration of the digital objects and the updating of the site would be ridiculously cumbersome.

Designated image databases

Assuming that a more structured approach is seen as desirable, it is possible to use an existing database programme to store the metadata and link it to the image files. One solution, for example, would be to use a standard desktop database system such as Microsoft Access or Filemaker Pro. Both will allow for the incorporation of, or linking to, multimedia objects such as images, and can interface relatively easily with the web (eg using Microsoft's Active Server Pages). However, again there are limitations as to how much control or complexity of description one can employ in the catalogue.

The second option is to choose a system designed specifically for image databases – an option that has been chosen by many projects. Numerous collection and image management systems have been developed and are readily available at present, such as iBase's inVisage system, and Willoughby's MultiMIMSY 2000 system (**http://www.willo.com**). iBase, for example, has been chosen as the system to back up the digital collections of the UK's new Tate Modern gallery in London. The advantage of this type of system is that it provides full web access and delivery, easy and secure cataloguing interfaces, and user/cataloguer searching and browsing utilities. Moreover, they claim to be secure and robust pieces of software. As an off-the-shelf solution, therefore, these can prove to be very attractive but they do have some drawbacks. The costs of purchasing and installing the software can be high, and the lack of interoperability with existing catalogues is noticeable. They are also clearly geared towards museums and galleries, focusing on images but restricted when it comes to text. Furthermore, although these systems claim to be XML-compliant (a phrase which can hide a multitude of sins), one has to be certain that this is indeed the case. A Rolls-Royce solution would be to use a proven mainframe database developer such as Oracle, who are currently marketing their 8i system and claiming it as the world's first Internet database. This software comes with almost complete flexibility and development potential, but comes at a price, and the implementation of the software would require considerable training and expertise.

Textbase searching

A third option that applies if one chooses the SGML/XML route is to treat the catalogue as a textbase. There is software developed in the SGML world which allows one to catalogue all the material in XML, place the XML file or files on a server, and allow the user to search these 'texts'. The user would probably do this with a web form. Then, through CGI scripts, the system could convert the user's input (ie the search or browse) to a syntax usable by the SGML/XML search engine on the server. This search engine in turn would analyse the catalogue files and return the hits, with a further set of scripts converting the material back into HTML for web display (although with XML this intermediate conversion process will eventually not be necessary). Experience has shown that this solution works well and is customizable to such an extent as to satisfy the most demanding of users (providing the appropriate metadata has been included). An illustration of this is provided in Figure 5.3. Here we can see the user interface is separated from the main server by 'middleware' (an intermediate system to act as a filter or for processing queries/results), whilst the other parties (cataloguers, administration and system support) can both enter and retrieve information through other interfaces.

The UK's Oxford Text Archive has been running such a system for several years now, using the OpenText 5.0 software to deliver searchable electronic texts, and this can easily be expanded to linking to multimedia objects such as images, audio and video (as witnessed in the Wilfred Owen Multimedia Digital Archive). This is not, however, the easiest solution to implement and requires staff knowledgeable in the software (both installation and maintenance), SGML/XML expertise, CGI scripting, support and a server (usually a dedicated UNIX server). This is in addition, of course, to the initial cost of the software itself.

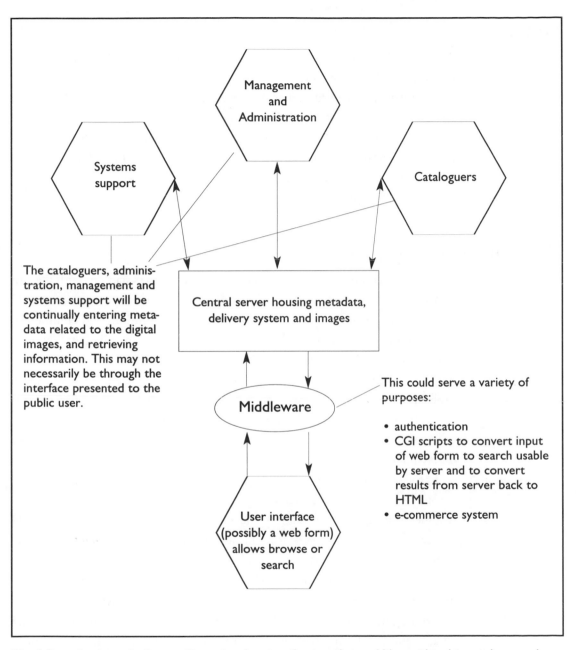

The cataloguers, adminis-
tration, management and
systems support will be
continually entering metadata related to the digital
images, and retrieving
information. This may not
necessarily be through the
interface presented to the
public user.

This could serve a variety of
purposes:

- authentication
- CGI scripts to convert input
  of web form to search usable
  by server and to convert
  results from server back to
  HTML
- e-commerce system

Fig. 5.3   *A schematic diagram illustrating the type of system that could be employed to catalogue and
deliver the images*

Outsourcing

As with digitization of the source material, another solution is to outsource the delivery of your archive. Large commercial-based image collections will offer to house and distribute third-party collections. An example of this is the Bridgeman Art Gallery in the UK (**http://www.bridgeman.co.uk/**), which acts as an agent for museums and galleries that do not wish to cover the delivery of their images. Their systems allow for browsing, searching and the selling of digital images. If entering into any agreement of this sort, however, one should be certain that the rights agreements are satisfactory.

What the user sees

Although it must be noted that not all digitization projects start out with the aim of actually delivering something to an end-user (preservation may be the sole aim), we can agree that the majority of them do. Institutions and commercial companies who run projects where this is a central concern will obviously want to exert some control over the users' access to the system. At the very least, one may wish to monitor the hits and build up a profile of current users; but more probably a project might allow users to get access to some versions of the images but might be reluctant to release all of them (especially high-quality files) freely to anyone. In other words, one will probably want to control what the user or different types of users can see.

At the same time, human computer interface (HCI) issues must be taken into account – in other words, what does the user *want* to see? The project system – whether web-based or standalone – must be easily usable. The catalogues should be searchable or at the very least browsable. This could range from simple searches to using Boolean operators, proximity searching and probabilistic retrieval. Navigation aids should be both intuitive and apparent, and consistency maintained throughout. There should be online help, and maybe even a facility for creating user profiles (saving searches for future visits). The interface should be aesthetically pleasing with an air of professionalism, but at the same time it should be open to accommodating the latest developments in technology, providing new tools and utilities to assist the user in their research. Finally, if the site is to involve some form of financial transaction (such as allowing the user to buy images online), then the e-commerce system used must be both straightforward and secure.

Before looking at a real-life example of all of this, one can make some general observations about the way many digital imaging projects present their collections to the end-user. Most obviously, any site of note will allow users to browse and search the catalogue that lies behind the image collection. In theory this will allow multiple access points to the same digital object, and it should be interoperable with other catalogues (especially if this is in a library setting, where it makes sense to integrate the digital image collection with the existing OPAC). When the user has entered a search term or browsed a category down to the item level, the system should return to the user meaningful but selected metadata about the object – in other words, it is often inappropriate for the user to be returned the full catalogue entry. Users can then select each return or 'hit' and see the expanded metadata for that object.

The first digital image the user sees is usually a *thumbnail* image – ie a small derivative of around 100 pixels high (or thereabouts) which has been created from a larger image. This thumbnail should be small enough (or of sufficiently low quality, eg a JPEG file of up to 40:1 compression) to allow it to download quickly, but at the same time it must convey meaningful graphical information about the full image itself. Again this will allow users to hone their research more quickly without having to load in larger (and thus slower) image files.

From the thumbnail the user could be allowed to download a working-quality image. The term 'quality' here is hard to define but this could, for example, mean:

• an image of sufficient resolution to allow basic research to proceed (eg suitable for users who are only interested in seeing the general content of the image, but not for users who wish to perform detailed image analysis on the file)
• an image in a commercially orientated archive that allows users to know that this is the file they wish to order.

Quite often this type of image is delivered at a resolution of 72 dpi (ie screen resolution) to fit on a low-end monitor of 640 X 480. Even at 24-bit colour, using a file format such as JPEG with its compression routines, an image like this would be less than 100 Kb in size and therefore well suited for web delivery.

Some difficulty arises when one considers the next level of image – one which would allow advanced study or analysis, or indeed a good-quality print output (eg 150–200 dpi). Not only would these files be considerably larger in terms of file size (and thus slower to network), but one may not be too keen to allow such images to be freely available. Given a reasonably good printer, for example, such files could be recreated on paper at extremely good quality. The decision a project manager would need to make (possibly in conjunction with the curators and/or publications departments) is whether user access to these high-quality images should be restricted in some way, such as by a password system, or whether at this level the images should have to be purchased. Either way, it is quite common for imaging projects to draw a line in terms of access between the working-quality images outlined earlier and these high-quality images. To present some idea of the images that this could offer, Figure 5.4 contains derivatives created from a section of a master image (originally captured at 300 dpi, 24-bit colour) of an early 20th-century manuscript. The three derivatives created are a thumbnail, a working-quality image (for screen display) and a high-quality image (possibly for printing).

Such issues are further complicated, though, by the use of pyramid file formats. As was noted in Chapter 3, these allow seamless access to high-quality images by allowing the user to zoom in on the graphic to increase its detail. This, unfortunately, is very difficult to control. Once again, the project will need to ask whether it is prepared to allow these files to be made freely available.

All of the solutions noted above will usually involve creating these derivatives from the master image (ie the highest-quality digital image available). These images, usually uncompressed, are of such high resolution that the resulting file sizes can be extremely large, and it would be rare for these to be made publicly available on a website. This is in part due to the fact that these images would allow the end-user to have their own copy of the master image (possibly for further reproduction), but also because moving these files across the network would be extremely slow.

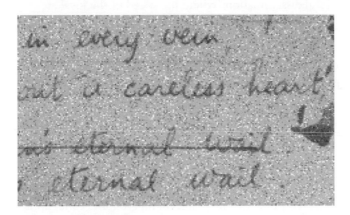

High-quality derivative: 150 dpi, 24-bit colour, TIFF, plus zoom in to 250%

Working-quality derivative: 72 dpi, 24-bit colour, JPEG, plus zoom in to 250%

Thumbnail derivative: 72 dpi, 100 pixels wide, JPEG, plus zoom in to 250%

Fig. 5.4   *Illustrating the degradation in quality between three derivatives*

When we think of delivering the files and attempting to satisfy the customer, we should not forget print delivery. In theory, a proper service may wish to consider delivering material via CD-ROM, e-mail, photographs, print output, fax or photocopying standard, as well as web access. We should also consider the charging systems that could be offered to the user. These may vary from subscriptions (such as are being offered by the AMICO project), to pay-per-use visits (eg buy an image at a time). Generally, most academic or non-profit-making projects tend to make this an equitable charging system, differentiating the prices charged for private as opposed to commercial use.

Before proceeding to a case study, it should be noted that the above discussions really only refer to remote access to the digital images. It is very common for host institutions to hold copies of even the master images on their own intranets for local dissemination (where the speed of the local area network will make delivery much quicker). Most notably this could be the case in a reading room in a library, or in a gallery, where the availability of master images would help deter requests to handle the original (assuming the room contained the necessary hardware and software to display the images).

Project Collage (http://collage.nhil.com)

This is a moderate-sized project (ie about 25,000 images) which provides a good example of a structured interface, dealing with all of the issues we have noted above. The project presents a digital image library of the collections at the Guildhall Library and Guildhall Art Gallery in London (funded by the Corporation of London). It is aimed at the general user interested in browsing the pictures, at the researcher and at raising income through sales of the images. The approach to the delivery system is interesting here. Project Collage commissioned iBase to develop a system according to their own specific requirements. They chose a self-contained production system that handled the metadata and images (linking the two automatically), and quickly established a controlled thesaurus for content description. They deliver the material via the web, but also with an option to order print surrogates. The system is based on barcodes, which assist in the administration of the images and the project management, and is an example of a total solution package covering the demands of the cataloguers, technicians, administrators and users. For the purposes of this discussion, however, it is the user interface which is most interesting.

To begin with, the user gains access to the site by a simple URL (**http://collage.nhil.com/**). The opening screen is pleasant and uncluttered, with a scattering of thumbnail images to make it more appealing. Immediately the user is faced with two options: a search box, and category headings for browsing. The latter (eg abstract ideas, natural world) takes the user to another page with further subheadings (eg military > military equipment > arms and armour). This in turn leads to a page full of thumbnails associated with that category, presenting nine or so images at a time. These thumbnails are presented as JPEGS, 120 pixels along the longest side, c 100 dpi, and compressed to a file size of around 4 Kb.

When users click on the thumbnail, they are taken to a larger version of the image with metadata describing its provenance and content. This second stage image is again a JPEG file, set at around 350 pixels along the long edge, with a resolution of 72 dpi. The file is compressed to a delivery size of 8 Kb. The user is offered an additional option of expanding the image once more to a final JPEG file, with the specifications of: c 700 pixels along the long edge, 72 dpi, and a file size of c 25 Kb. File naming is based on a system of *fileid*t.jpg, *fileid*r.jpg and *fileid*x.jpg, the *fileid* being a unique identifier for the file reflecting its shelfmark, with 't' applying to the thumbnail, 'r' to the medium version and 'x' to the larger version.

At this point the user cannot see any higher-quality images. To do so, they must place an order. Helpful information about postage and packaging is made explicit, as are details about the printing service. Ordering can take place online (using a pro-forma invoicing system) or by printing out a paper form.

As mentioned before, users can choose to search the collection (the results being displayed as a series of thumbnails), but they can also browse further category headings and thematic trails (eg Tudor London). It was mentioned earlier that online image collections may wish to use more advanced features to attract and help users, and Collage is no different in this as it employs a shopping basket facility and provides the option to download free wallpapers for desktop machines.

Project Collage is by no means the most sophisticated system available but it is a straightforward example that illustrates many of the issues discussed. More complicated systems are available and readers interested in doing their own survey should look to such examples as the Getty Images site, CORBIS (**http://www.corbis.com/**) or the Bridgeman Art Library itself.

Delivering full text

Up to now this book has focused on producing image files derived from the master copy (eg JPEGs/GIFs from TIFFs). However, many projects involved in the digitization of images that contain textual material are also interested in delivering full text to assist in searching and browsing. Two types of projects are typical in this respect:

1   The creation of digital images which are then used to produce machine-readable text; the original images can then be dispensed of as they are of no value.
2   As above, but then the original graphics are retained as facsimiles, the aim being to use the machine-readable text as the search backbone, allowing the user to look for particular words or phrases, with the results linking directly to the appropriate page images. Here the full text is being used to expand the search potential offered by standard metadata.

We can quickly come up with examples of both types of projects. If one were dealing with ephemeral material, for example, where there was no intrinsic value in the page image itself (eg grey literature projects), then the first scenario would be appropriate. The project manager would create the images of the pages, derive machine-readable text from the images using one of the two methods described below, and then focus upon delivering the text to the end-user. Methodologies for the delivery of text bases can be found in the large electronic text initiatives such as the Oxford Text Archive (see especially Morrison, Popham, and Wikander, 2000), and the electronic text centres at the Universities of Virginia and Michigan. Interestingly, all have settled on using SGML/XML as the means of delivering full text to the user in a browsable and searchable fashion. This is also the case with numerous commercially driven projects such as Chadwyck-Healey's Literature On-Line service.

The University of Virginia also hosts several projects where full text is used to link back to page image (namely a facsimile of the document), as in the second scenario above. Many other projects adopt this approach, such as the JSTOR initiative, or the forthcoming Early English Books On-line enterprise. The retention of the image is particularly important when dealing with documents that retain inherent value in their physical appearance (such as rare or unique items) and those which are so complex they go beyond the capabilities of current mark-up systems (or where the time and effort needed to record all the information using an encoding system would be prohibitive).

In terms of a workflow the first step is the creation of the page images themselves. We have already dealt extensively with this topic in previous chapters, but we should note here that at the benchmarking stage the resolutions have to be set to such a level as to capture the smallest font size on the page so that it can be subsequently read and used by further software (eg optical character readers). Once the page images have been created, one then needs to derive the machine-readable text from them (usually full text, ie every word on the page). There are two ways in which this can be done:

1   Transcription: using the page images, other surrogates, or possibly even the source documents themselves, the material is transcribed and recorded into a simple text processor. In the majority of cases this is recorded and saved as plain text. Like digitization, this is frequently outsourced to an external agency. Throughput for this depends to some extent on the nature of the source document, but primarily on the typists' speed – greatly reduced, of course, if they are being asked to insert encoding at the same time.

2   Optical character recognition (OCR): this is a similar approach to CBIR, but with considerably better results. Using a series of algorithms, OCR software can be run over digital images (usually TIFF files) and machine-readable text can be derived from them. The question here is one of accuracy. The nature of the original source document, and the quality (and language) of the typefaces used, will all have a direct effect on how accurate the OCR is. This is usually presented as a percentage, such as 98% accuracy, which would imply only two characters in every 100 are considered incorrect. The standard software used for OCR at present is OmniPage Pro,

though this is not particularly suitable for non-Roman characters. At the University of Michigan, for example, an array of CPUs is used simply to OCR page images and produce machine-readable text. With five CPUs linked together, they can process 3–5000 pages a day at an average of 3000 characters a page. As with keying in, OCRing can also be outsourced to an external agency.

Commonly held views on the potential throughput of OCR are often wildly optimistic. If one were scanning and then OCRing using a straightforward flatbed scanner, then one would expect a throughput of only around 30 A4 pages an hour at the maximum. However, OCR software often has a facility for batch processing of previously created image files, which will greatly increase the throughput.

Whatever strategy is adopted, the project will end up with a full-text machine-readable version of the source document(s). If it is decided that 100% accuracy is required, then further proof-reading and quality assurance checks will need to be performed. This could be an expensive process; it is one of the truisms of OCRing that the first pass – the capturing – is relatively cheap, but the second pass, in which the tidying up of the material is done, is always more expensive. However, many projects cannot afford these costs, and indeed use the OCRed full text as an addition to standard cataloguing for locating the page images. In this case uncorrected OCR (or 'dirty OCR') is often employed. Here, the OCR software is run over the page images and the full text it produces is used, in the full knowledge that it is probably not 100% accurate. This will be less of a concern, though, if the end-user is really only interested in the digital facsimile. An example of such a project is the Internet Library of Early Journals, which uses uncorrected OCR text purely as an assist to locating page images.

Two other solutions should be mentioned, however. The first relates to Adobe's PDF system, which allows the simple distribution and searching of facsimile-style documents. PDF also allows for built-in functions such as zooming in on the text. However, as noted in an earlier chapter, if the source document was not 'born' electronic, then the files resulting from a conversion can be prohibitively large. Furthermore, this also requires the user to have an Acrobat Reader installed on their machine. The second solution is a similar approach, this time using TIFF files instead of creating PDF documents, and is known as smart image technology (SIT). It works by using digital facsimiles of the pages, applying OCR algorithms to them, and then linking the OCR-derived index to the images automatically, and in particular to the specific word or phrase on the page. Users can then enter search terms and will be returned with their results as part of the digital facsimile. Ramot Digital Resources, the business wing of Tel Aviv University, has developed a system called IOTA which is worth examining.

Assuming one does not pursue the PDF or SIT route, the final step in this process is to deliver the machine-readable text, linked to the page images if appropriate, to the user. The searching and analysis of texts by computers is decades old and has produced numerous discussions and systems. Rather than repeat these arguments, it is reasonable simply to suggest here the currently most commonly adopted solution. Once the full text has been created (either by transcription or by OCR), it is saved as plain unformatted ASCII text. This is then surrounded with some form of structural mark-up using a recognized SGML DTD (eg the TEI), with the level of encoding to be chosen by the project manager. This text can then be embedded as part of the overall metadata for the collection, which can be searched using the options outlined above. If using the SGML/XML approach, the images can be linked to the metadata by straightforward cross-referencing methods.

Copyright and image protection (watermarking)

We have already briefly discussed copyright in earlier chapters. For example, one of the first questions when developing the decision matrix in Chapter 2, was whether the material proposed for conversion was still in copyright. If it was, then the next question to ask is whether the rights to use the material were secured or could be secured. Similarly, in the ready reckoner for digitization costs, we included a reference to the possible costs that could be accrued when attempting to clear rights, covering the time involved and the fee one may have to pay to the rights holders.

Yet to the project manager copyright works both ways: on the one hand, institutions involved in digitization need to be certain that they are operating within the law when it comes to capturing material, but the other side of the coin is that they will also want to feel that there is some attempt being made to safeguard their own rights when the images are eventually delivered. In other words, they will want to make sure that someone does not reproduce their images without first seeking permission (a particular concern if the project depends upon an income stream generated from the sale of the images). Such fears are realistic, highlighted by recent cases such as Corel v Bridgeman, where images from the Bridgeman Art Library were reproduced without permission by Corel on a CD-ROM. Alarmingly, the Art Library lost the case, causing much concern in the US (although the ruling has little relevance in other countries).

Dealing with the first aspect – the right to use material – there are two simple questions one needs to ask that apply world-wide:

- is the material that one wishes to use still in copyright?
- if it is, who owns the copyright?

The answer to the first question will vary from country to country as the law varies considerably internationally. Thus in the UK it would be illegal to digitize a volume of Siegfried Sassoon's poetry because the text itself is still in copyright (as Sassoon died in 1967), but in the US volumes of his poetry dating from the 1920s do appear on websites, quite legally, because the law in the USA points to the original date of publication, not the death of the author. Therefore any global attempt to define the law is impossible as it varies so much internationally. The nearest thing to a commonality of copyright law is the present EU Draft Directive which is aiming to set a legal standard for members of the European Community. This is still under discussion at the time of writing, though the common agreement for this was announced on 7 June 2000.

Having recognized the problems of the international variations in the law, it is still possible to make a few general observations. First, objects themselves can have multiple rights owners, which means that all of these will have to be cleared. Reproducing an image in a book of a manuscript could involve clearing the rights with the original author of the text contained in the facsimile, the photographer who reproduced the document for inclusion in the book, and the typesetter or publishing house. In theory one may have to contact all three parties to use the item legitimately.

This brings us on to the question of who owns the rights. Leaving aside the problem of multiple ownership, the next major problem is actually finding the names and contact addresses of the rights holders, corresponding with them and coming to some form of agreement. This is often extremely difficult and time-consuming (hence its addition in the ready reckoner). Furthermore, there is no set fee that people charge for the use of a single image. This can vary from no charge to hundreds of pounds, and the price will increase the wider you wish to disseminate the image (eg world rights usually cost more than national distribution rights).

It is not surprising, therefore, that many digital imaging projects concentrate on material they own the rights to, or on items out of copyright. As can be seen in the selection and assessment matrix in Chapter 2, it is suggested that if the rights cannot be secured with ease, the project could be stopped there and then. However, for many projects this is simply not an option, as the collections policy may dictate that for the project to be completed some items that are currently in copyright will have to be used. In this scenario, then, it is worth noting the following general recommendations, which will hopefully assist in clearing copyright:

1   When trying to find the rights holders, use existing tools to hand such as contact details for the original publisher, standard directories of artists, authors, and maybe even telephone directories and registers of births or deaths. Some projects have even advertised in appropriate journals. If this fails, try national bodies that may hold the information (eg in the UK, one could use the Copyright Licensing Agency, but internationally services such as Copywatch may also help).

2   If you still cannot find the copyright holder but need to use the image, then include a disclaimer. If the copyright holder does appear, then you can at least offer to remove the material. However, this involves some risk of being drawn into a legal action. Therefore it is usually recommended that projects do not publish material in any form for which there is no recorded permission to do so from the copyright holder. Do not assume that there is such a thing as 'fair use' until this has been clarified under national law. Furthermore, do not assume that no response from the holder in effect

permits the use of material – it does not.

3   It is essential that the project should keep a record of all correspondences and attempts to clear copyright (usually called a diligence file), and any agreement reached should be recorded in writing. An administrative database system to keep track of the stage of copyright agreements can be very helpful.

4   If you have identified a large collection that the project would like to use, then approach the holding institution with the suggestion of becoming joint partners in the project. State-funded institutions are often very keen to participate in projects.

5   When contacting the rights holder, try to cover all the instances in which the material may be used (this will save time in reapplying for rights in the future).

6   Where the project is an academic non-profit-making initiative, indicate this in the initial letter. However, you should also state that the project is willing to make a financial contribution for the material, stressing of course that funds are limited. Offer to include an acknowledgement of the rights holder's choosing (usually a link to their website).

7   Be honest. If the project plans to disseminate the material via the web, then say so and be prepared to pay world rights. However, use the strength of the Internet as an advantage, saying that this is, in effect, profile-raising and free advertising.

8   Never underestimate the time it will take to clear copyright. Writing letters, chasing names and addresses, waiting for replies and reaching agreements can all take months to complete.

Once a project has begun to disseminate images, it is important to have some form of control over their subsequent use, and more importantly misuse. As Oppenheim (1999, 40) notes:

> Once something has been electrocopied, any person could send it around the world to thousands or millions of people with trivial effort. This, of course, would lead to loss of sales of the original materials by the publisher. Furthermore, the copies would be perfect, it would cost the perpetrator

virtually nothing to do this copying, and such actions would be difficult if not impossible to police.

The restricted access system outlined earlier is a straightforward way to draw a line between what users can get for free and what they will need to request directly (and possibly pay for). However, once they do get copies of the digital files, how can one attempt to limit future misuse? Even with free working-quality images, one may need to be careful, as in theory a user could download all of these and mount an alternative site. Simply relying on the fact that this is illegal is not generally acceptable to most institutions, and most digital imaging projects will wish to employ a more developed system to try to deter this type of action.

The simplest method is to always include an agreed copyright statement and guidelines for usage on whatever medium is used for delivery. For a website, for example, there can be an opening screen on which the user has to agree to abide by certain rules before proceeding to view the images. In many ways this is exactly the same as the type of printed form issued by standard reprographic units to restrict subsequent use.

In addition, many projects insert banners or captions into the image itself (usually along the border of the image). This could be as simple as '©Museum of Wessex' but could also be more elaborate, depending on the wishes of the institution. These captions can be captured at the digitization stage, but more probably will be automatically added as part of any post-processing, using software such as Adobe Photoshop, which will allow for a batch insertion. Some file formats (such as TIFF) allow for textual copyright information to be inserted as part of the metadata linked to the image and stored in the header, and would thus not be visible on screen unless brought up by the imaging software. However, in both cases this information can be removed quite easily, either by cropping the image, or by simply deleting the metadata.

One could also elect to encrypt all images, only releasing the encryption key to legitimate users. Yet the most elaborate system available at the moment is that adding a digital watermark. In essence the term *watermark* in this context refers to a pattern of bits inserted into a digital image that identifies copyright information about the file. Digital watermarks are often invisible to the user, although not always, and are dispersed throughout the file in such a way that they cannot be altered. Furthermore, they are able to withstand normal changes to the file, to the extent that if the file is printed out and then rescanned, the watermark will still be there. To view a watermark, one requires a special program that knows how to extract and display the watermark information. A good example of what is on offer can be seen in the system developed by the Digimarc Corporation (**http://www.digimarc.com**).

Watermarking, in theory, provides a better system for protecting your images. In addition to the advantages noted above:

1   It will help to remind people who owns the rights to the image, thus helping to prevent accidental misuse of images (they are often displayed automatically in a separate window by image-processing software).
2   It can be automated and added on the fly.
3   It allows specialized companies to perform a web-sweeping service to track current use and appearance of the images, hence the term digital *fingerprinting*. These can allow for such sophisticated auditing systems as knowing when the file was downloaded and by whom (eg via a user ID if this is utilized, or by the IP address of the client machine).

However, at the same time, there are notable problems with watermarking:

1   The systems employed at the moment are far from stable.
2   It can be a costly business, not only for the software but also for centrally registering the information relating to the watermarks.
3   Watermarks can, with some difficulty, be removed.
4   Even the presence of the watermark will not stop the determined misuser of the image from infringing copyright.

An even more interesting issue is that should misuse of an image be identified, what the next step would be. Apart from a polite request to remove the image and cease its distribution, there is very little one can realistically do, as the costs of mounting any legal action (especially an international one) are prohibitive and the likelihood of success is far from certain. How one protects images, then, is a matter of choice. Given time and money, watermarking may well be worth investigating, but if resources are limited then a banner approach may be the best one can hope for, coupled with a restrictive access policy to certain levels of quality.

Banners and watermarks can be made to be intrusive – for example, they can cut right across the image and be always visible. Some people consider this to be a good thing as it acts as a constant reminder to the user and makes misrepresentation more difficult. However, others see this as defeating the entire purpose of the digital imaging project, namely to increase full access to the objects.

Copyright and image protection decisions will have to be made at an institutional level, and again will draw in expertise from other possible sectors. It would be worthwhile, particularly in a larger project, to have access to legal advice concerning copyright issues, which could also be called upon should a case of misuse be discovered. Larger projects may also be interested in seeing if there are any electronic copyright management systems (ECMS) they could use, which can help not only in restricting access but also in collecting royalties. These are particularly useful if the rights for the material are held by many different institutions.

In summary, then, the access to the images and the image protection system that is chosen should take into consideration the concerns of departments that might be affected by this. Many institutions have their own reprographics service that sells images directly to users via traditional photography, possibly even through a shop. How will their interests be protected? Furthermore, curators of the material are rightly concerned that images are used correctly – ie they are not distorted, titled incorrectly or used inappropriately. Again, will the image protection system satisfy their needs as well?

Archiving and preservation

Archiving is a big issue, particularly in academic research libraries. Such libraries acquire print-on-paper, secure in the knowledge that such materials will continue to be available in fifty years' time. No such security of thought can be present in the digitization process. Technology changes too fast, with hardware and software becoming obsolescent very quickly.

(Ayris, 1998)

Despite Ayris's observations, all of which are true, one of the most alarming features of many digital imaging projects that were conducted throughout the 1990s is the way the archiving of the project's components was overlooked. Gould and Ebdon (1999), for example, note that nearly half of the libraries they surveyed that were involved in digitization did not have a policy for migrating data. Sometimes only single copies of files were saved, occasionally in a proprietary format that is now unusable. These files are often dispersed and disorganized; showing an overall disregard for many of the practices built up in both the archiving world and the IT sector.

Michael Day (1999) notes three possible solutions to preserving digital information:

- technology preservation (ie maintaining a museum of machines and software)
- emulation (that is to say, using up-to-date hardware to attempt to recreate the original operating conditions)
- migration.

The last of these involves transferring files from one piece of hardware/software/file format to another. Increasingly, this is being seen as the most realistic and achievable way of attempting to preserve digital data. In a sense, then, this is different from traditional archiving approaches, where the source document is touched as little as possible. In digital archiving, there is a need for continual 'touches' (albeit virtual).

It is the responsibility of the project manager to ensure that the digital images and associated files are successfully archived and actively monitored. At the beginning of this book, we noted that digitization projects can be extremely expensive in terms of time and money. It would therefore be highly unacceptable to have to repeat the project after a few years simply because the archiving strategy was incorrect, or indeed non-existent.

When considering a correct strategy one has to be certain that certain objectives have been met:

1   The files that are being saved must be the correct ones, and form a complete record of the project (eg save all master images and derivatives, plus associated metadata files). For example, if some form of post-editing is being performed on the master images, one may decide to back-up the images that come straight from the scanner (which may be considered more 'authentic'), and then the master images with slight modifications. Again, the file-naming structure needs to be worked out beforehand.

2   The files must be saved in a non-proprietary format – eg as TIFFs, with the metadata exported to plain text files. Most importantly for master images, the files should be saved with no compression (or lossless compression) and should avoid interpolation.

3   At least three distinct copies of all the files should have been made on a permanent storage system (such as magnetic disks) and kept in disparate locations (this is known as *replication*).

4   An active policy should have been instigated to refresh the archived copies (remembering that all storage mediums have a shelf life), and to migrate them to new emerging standard formats as they appear. The file-naming system adopted by the project must be able to reflect this.

5   To assist in all of this, the technical and administrative metadata developed by the project should record the appropriate information (using the recommendations of such projects as the CEDARS or NEDLIB initiatives, and the Council on Library and Information Resources' analysis of the risk factors associated with migration).

It is the role of the project manager, in conjunction with the project administrators and technical experts, to see that all of the above are met and that there are systems in place to make sure these continue.

The complete life-cycle of a digital imaging project

Steve Chapman (1998) correctly points out that 'digital images do not make themselves.' More importantly, this could be emended to read 'digital projects do not make themselves.' Throughout this book it has been stressed that digitization is a team activity, drawing on the resources and expertise of many constituent parts. At the heart of this team is the project manager: the person responsible for seeing the project through from cradle to grave and beyond (ie its continued maintenance and preservation). Project managers must ensure that it ties in with institutional strategies, and that the project finishes *on time* and *within budget*. They are frequently asked to manage several projects at a time – ie a whole cross-collection digitization initiative – and to interface these into existing systems (both electronic and print) in what is known as a hybrid approach.

How can one attempt to achieve such difficult goals? This penultimate section will offer some advice to the project manager, drawing together the aspects of the life-cycle of a digitization project already listed, and adding a few more strategic steps. The life-cycle of a digitization project has been touched on throughout this book, but perhaps it is worthwhile now to begin to draw this all together. It has been the norm in previous chapters to use hypothetical examples to illustrate the points made earlier. However, this time we will draw on a real-life example – that of the large journal-digitization project, JSTOR (**http://www.jstor.ac.uk** or **http://www.jstor.org**). This is an internationally renowned resource of considerable value to researchers and scholars, offering full-text searching of journals with results linked to facsimile images. It began in 1995 initiated by the Andrew W Mellon Foundation. However, bearing in mind the issues raised above relating to OCR, archiving and delivery, what could we perceive as the exact steps in the workflow of the JSTOR project? In effect these can be summarized in the terms given in Table 5.1, cross-referenced to those used in this book to describe the various stages of a project.

The steps discussed in this book are all present in Table 5.1. However, up to now the impression has perhaps been that a project moves through each stage one at a time. Yet the JSTOR example illustrates that several activities go on concurrently (eg cataloguing carries on throughout the project, and there are two noted stages of quality assurance checks).

Table 5.1

Stage		Workflow criterion
1	Target journal	Selection/assessment
2	Define Journal (two FTE librarians research the title, the bibliographic information and history etc).	Preparation
3	Collect full run of journal (publishers are meant to supply these, but quite often the librarians will have to seek out missing editions in other collections).	Preparation
4	Assemble material at JSTOR (librarians look over journal to check it, work out the intellectual structure, generally sampling about 5–10 volumes closely at various points throughout the full back-run).	Preparation
5	Analyse and prepare material (check the type of material contained in the journal, eg charts, photographs, landscape/portrait, level of print, TOC).	Preparation
6	Production analysis (production technician will review every page of each issue recording in a database such information as pagination, graphics, intellectual features, scanning problems etc).	Digitization assessment
7	Database print-out (all the information above is printed out and acts as a scanning guideline for the external vendor).	Digitization assessment/cataloguing
8	Send to vendor.	Preparation/outsourcing
9	Vendor keyboards in metadata.	Cataloguing
10	Vendor scans in images (600 dpi bi-tonal TIFFs, or 200 dpi greyscale/colour JPEGs) – TIFFs are compressed and delivered in the final version as GIFs (converted on the fly).	Digitization/creating derivatives
11	OCR text using TypeReader.	Delivering full text/OCR
12	Correct OCR to a 1:2000 error rate.	Quality assurance/proof-reading
13	Write to CD-ROM and deliver back to JSTOR.	Archiving/delivery
14	JSTOR performs automatic check on resolution, then samples 10% and quality-checks images and OCR; 100% indexing of all material.	Quality assurance
15	Archive material to tape and then mirrored at Princeton and Manchester.	Archiving/delivery
16	Deliver (via a server at University of Michigan, based on an Access flat-file database abstracted by an FTL search engine linking metadata to image).	Delivery

In a sense this heightens the responsibility of the project manager, as he or she will have to make sure that all of these aspects are coordinated and delivered on time. Paul Ayris (1998) has produced a short decision matrix to support digitization projects, posing questions under the following headings: assessment, gains, standards, administrative issues. Most of these are covered in the decision matrix outlined in Chapters 2 and 3, but for now it is worth considering the questions that focus on the administration or project management side of the initiative:

- Do you have enough money?
- Have copyright and rights issues been secured?
- Does your institution have enough expertise?
- Is there a partnership with a commercial provider?
- Do the benefits justify the costs?

The first question is one every manager will have to deal with. In Chapter 4 we looked at the cost of digitization and mentioned that such unit costs could be trebled if the whole project is to be completed. But this does not answer the question of where the money comes from in the first place.

Any new digitization project will incur initial capital and start-up costs for which money will need to be sought. In some instances, outside funding agencies may be prepared to cover these with project grants, but this is not always the case and some internal funding may have to be sought. Thereafter, subsequent digitization initiatives may be able to draw on already purchased equipment and share the overheads, thus reducing their overall costs, but at the same time hardware will have to be housed, operated and supported, and more worryingly will be depreciating all the time, requiring new equipment to be purchased. It is of course possible to generate income from the sale of digital images (or print derivatives produced from digital masters) but this in turn increases the overall administration costs.

Assuming, though, that funding has been secured, and a steady income stream predicted (either through recurrent grants or sales), the project manager will have to make sure that the finances can be stretched to cover all costs. This will be a combination of looking at the project's overall aims, assessing the staffing and/or outsourcing costs, planning the project as a series of deliverables and milestones (perhaps using Gantt charts), and assigning appropriate resources. Project managers will have to put in place a system for monitoring the progress of the project, through team meetings and regular reports.

Most importantly, they will have to coordinate the activities of all parties involved in the project. This can, to a certain degree, be eased by using a centralized cataloguing system. Not only will this produce coordinated metadata, but it will allow the administrator and the manager to check quickly on the progress and status of each digital file. We have already noted that off-the-shelf packages such as iBase can be customized to produce overall management systems, but even if that option has not been pursued, the manager should devise some standard checklists to allow the assessors, cataloguers and digitizers to record all the information they need to about the source document or the digital file, and to indicate its progress in the project. For example, when it comes to ordering images the step-by-step approach might be:

1   The customer sends in an initial request to the administration department, stating the exact order.
2   The administration sees if a digital file already exists.
3   If one does, they will issue a pro-forma invoice. If there is no digital file, then the order will necessitate assessing the object and making a copyright check before the invoice is issued.
4   The customer returns the payment and agrees to any copyright restrictions imposed by the service.
5   The image is then distributed, or if it is a new item, captured and then sent to the customer.
6   The administration logs the order.

Similarly during the actual capture stage the digitizer may be asked to complete a form along the following lines:

1   Has benchmarking been successfully carried out? YES/NO (If YES, record here the exact details of the recommended scan settings: capture device, capture software, resolution, bit-depth, file format).

2   Has the scanning system been calibrated? YES/NO (If YES, make a note of all settings).

3   On digitizing the source material, record all settings: capture device, capture software, resolution, bit–depth, file format, file name (in accordance with agreed naming system), dimensions of images (X and Y axis).

4   Have QA checks been performed on the digital image? YES/NO (this in turn should lead to a separate checklist).

5   Are modifications needed? YES/NO (If YES, record problems and suggested modifications).

In both scenarios it is assumed that most monitoring will be performed electronically and fed into a central system. We are following here the workflows outlined in previous chapters, but this time posing questions for the individual team member (ie the digitizer or the administrator) to answer. By completing this type of form, and recording the appropriate details, he or she is in fact not only recording information that will feed directly into the metadata for the digital image (automatically, one would hope), but also monitoring the progress of the operation.

Bringing this together we can finalize the workflow for the digital imaging project shown in Figure 5.5. One should note here the continued reference to the workflows established in previous chapters during this book. These should be used accordingly.

At the beginning of this section it was noted that a digitization project generally consists of several key personnel – in other words, it involves a team of staff. Apart from the project manager, then, exactly who might these other personnel be? The simple answer to this is anyone needed to complete the project successfully, regardless of whether they are working full-time on the project or just offering advice. In this sense, then, it is perhaps better to identify key roles and responsibilities that need to be covered. In terms of the tasks identified throughout this book, we could describe a structure as including:

• a *central section* (management, administration, liaising with external vendors, clearing copyright, e–commerce and marketing)

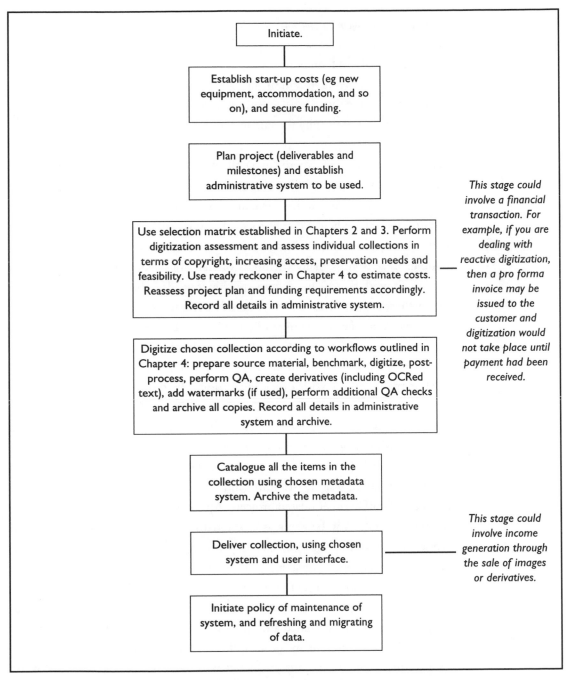

Fig. 5.5   *The final workflow for the digital imaging project*

- a *data management section* (cataloguing, metadata advice, expertise on preservation and conservation, preparation of material)
- a *systems section* (IT support, system maintenance, archiving and preservation)
- a *digitization service* (digitization assessment, benchmarking, digital conversion, quality assurance, creating electronic and print-based derivatives, traditional photography for surrogates).

Here we have a team of experts, or a collection of expertise, all of which may be needed to complete a digital imaging project successfully. Undoubtedly some of these may already be to hand, or several areas may be covered by a single member of staff (especially when it comes to smaller projects), but more often than not they will require new staff, new hardware and software, accommodation, and training. Exactly how many members of staff are needed depends entirely on how much work there is to do, how quickly it needs to be done, and how much money there is to draw upon. One can only point to examples elsewhere as some indicators. A good example might be the Digital Library Production Services at the University of Michigan. Here they have developed an efficient production line to digitize large collections held in the University, and to partake in collaborative ventures with other institutions. In terms of staffing, Michigan employ an overall head of services, five members of staff involved in *data management* (interface specialist, data loading and duplication, OCRing and database maintenance), six members of staff in *systems* (SGML encoding, numerical data, programming, further database support), two-and-a-half members of staff in *imaging* (scanning and post-processing), and four-and-a-half members of staff in other related projects. Although the structure of the DLPS at Michigan should not be seen as a standard, and indeed the numbers and responsibilities of the staff may change over time, this does give an indication that, to run a fully operational digitization service that can handle large quantities of data, one is looking to staff numbers of around 15 or so. This is, of course, a major undertaking for any institution (particularly when one remembers that equipment has to be purchased and supported, and accommodation found for a team of this size), but many projects have found when embarking on such ventures that some of the staff (or to put it another way a large amount of the expertise needed) are already in place. Digitization services *can fit* into existing departments and draw on others for guidance and expertise. In other words, they do not have to be 'green-field developments' in every case.

The Utopian vision

It is fitting to end this book with a basis for future discussion. Throughout the previous chapters we have mentioned the decisions that need to be made, the expertise that should be involved and so on. A fruitful way to bring this all together in a final summary is to paint a hypothetical vision of an ideal digitization service. We will base this at the University of Wessex (fictitious), but this time allow the institution to have substantial resources at its disposal (this is Utopia after all).

Assuming that the collections held at the University of Wessex are numerous, let us assume that the institution wants to digitize as many of its collections as it can. Faced with this prospect, the institution sets itself the aim of creating a world-class digital library, and becoming a forerunner in the field. In this ideal world the mission statement of such an initiative could be:

> To provide the scholars and students at the University of Wessex, and beyond, access to as many high-quality digital resources as possible to assist in their teaching and research.

With this in mind the digital initiative would be:

1   Hybrid: it will link to existing print and digital collections, and their catalogues (including the university's OPAC, the networked CD-ROMs and web subscriptions, and to other remote services), and will bear in mind future linking other similar initiatives in external institutions.
2   Sustainable: it will attract funding through external grants, and also via e-commerce by the sale of digital and print surrogates.
3   Suited to accommodating the needs of reactive digitization (ie ideally, to providing an on-demand digitization service for readers), but at the same time it would be proactive in targeting collections.

To accomplish this, we would need to draw together all the lessons learnt in this book so far. In so doing we can map out a step-by-step approach to achieving these goals:

1   The project manager should actively survey the community in the institution, using the questionnaires in Appendix B. This will allow one to identify:
    • all previous and ongoing digitization projects
    • all collections that could be potentially digitized
    • current policies and infrastructures.

2   This should be followed by a user survey canvassing views and opinions from readers, customers and other interested parties. To accompany this a traditional research exercise should be conducted using the further reading in Appendix C and any other studies of digital imaging projects in order to get an up-to-date view of the most recent developments. The manager should draw this together in a brief report providing a synopsis of the current situation locally and externally.

3   Taking these findings into account, one could then begin to identify notable gaps in the hardware presently available (both traditional cameras and digitization equipment). This could then be prioritized for future purchases. Collections will vary from institution to institution, but most larger initiatives will need access to a good range of hardware, such as flatbed scanners, sheet-feeders, microform scanners, 35-mm slide scanners, high-level digitization cameras or scanbacks, and open-book scanners. In addition they will need to be able to make film surrogates (to pursue an internegative approach if needed), and a range of printers to produce good output.

4   The manager will need to hire additional staff to begin to assess the collections identified in the survey. They in turn can use the decision matrix developed in Chapters 2 and 3. The collections should then be prioritized according to the three categories (access, preservation, feasibility) and the digitization assessments for each will be recorded.

5   Potential demand for the digital images could be identified using the above surveys (plus previous records of user requests). The manager can then present a business model for the service that can meet both reactive and

proactive needs. In this outline an initial stage should be outlined that will allow for limited throughput to begin with, but this will offer the chance to test and refine all the systems. Yet the model should also outline a 'full production' infrastructure. Most importantly this business plan should include:

- hardware and software needed, including depreciation and maintenance costs
- set-up costs, accommodation, overheads, transport and so on
- *central section staff* – manager(s), administration support, legal consultancy, marketing support
- *data management staff* – manager, preservation and conservation consultancy, cataloguers
- *systems staff* – manager, IT support at various levels, archiving specialists
- *digitization service staff* – manager, camera operators (digital and film), OCR expertise
- a clearly defined management structure and line of reporting
- projected costings and revenue streams.

6   The metadata system that is to be used (probably based on XML) should be finalized including the file-naming structures. This should be interoperable with existing catalogues and allow multiple points of access for the user. Furthermore, the full workflows and administrative systems need to be established, as will the system architecture to bring all three together.

7   Begin small: employ enough staff to start work on developing a reactive service integrating with any existing services. In the beginning, aim to process only a small number of requests but to document everything. Furthermore, begin to target a few collections that were prioritized as scoring high on 'increased access', but which will also be representative of the types of material that may arise in the future. Use these examples to test all the workflows, the benchmarking and QA tests, the hardware and software, and the administrative and metadata systems. Evaluate all of these and be prepared to alter them according to any findings. You should then begin to assemble a portfolio of digital images taken from various source materials and at various resolutions to allow speedier assessments in the future. Furthermore, you should start to look at external digitization

agencies, as these may need to be called upon in the future. Finally, start to employ the remaining staff needed to begin work on the delivery system and the user interface.

8   The project should then start to run trials on the overall archiving system, rigorously testing in controlled conditions the refreshing and migration strategies settled on earlier (and make any alterations if needed).

9   The delivery and user interface systems should be finalized after you have performed a full evaluation of these with selected users. Ideally this will allow for web access, with free thumbnails and working-quality images. In keeping with standard practices, you should probably restrict access to the higher-quality images (and print copies), but develop an automated system which allows for online ordering of derivatives.

10 After an appropriate time, you should begin to ramp up production. More staff will be needed to accomplish the 'full' service (as described in the earlier business model). As each item is digitized, it will need to be catalogued and to go into the central image stock, thus allowing the collection to grow. Digitization will be initiated by reader requests, project level requests and proactive targeting of collections identified earlier.

11 The system can now be considered as being in full production mode. However, it can only survive if funds are secured and it has a rolling programme of expansion and collection development. To do this any funding opportunities will need to be pursued. Furthermore, a system that will allow for new collections to be proposed should be set up. The manager will need to monitor all the procedures outlined above to see if they can be improved. It is also advisable that a programme of rotating staff between the various jobs is initiated (allowing for career development and spreading the base of expertise). Staff should also be allowed to devote time to research and development.

Conclusion

In this final chapter we have attempted to draw all the previous discussions together by looking at the overall life-cycle of the digital imaging project. In particular we have focused on:

- cataloguing the digital images (CBIR compared with the text-based approach)
- metadata systems including SGML and XML
- delivery systems (namely dedicated databases and textbases)
- Project Collage (an example of an on-line digital imaging project)
- delivering full-text projects
- copyright
- archiving
- the full project and possible staffing structures for a digitization team.

The remainder of this book provides details of international digital imaging projects (in Appendix A), a series of questionnaires to be used in surveying potential digitization activity within your institution (Appendix B) and a select reading list for further study (Appendix C).

Appendix A
The national and international context of digitization

It is appropriate for this book to include a consideration of the main national and international projects that have been undertaken so far. The 1990s, to the librarian at the very least, could be termed the 'decade of digitization'. Countless millions of pounds, dollars, francs and marks have been ploughed into digital projects that have involved the conversion of library, museum and archive collections. It is no coincidence that this has gone hand in hand with the development of the world wide web, the final piece of the jigsaw needed to solve the problem of increasing access to cultural resources.

Beginning with the United Kingdom, it is clear that over the past decade funding for such initiatives has been generous to say the least. In the UK, the main sources of money have been the Joint Information Systems Committee (**http://www.jisc.ac.uk**), the Leverhulme Trust (**http://www.leverhulme. org.uk/**), the British Academy (**http://britac3.britac.ac.uk/**), the Arts and Humanities Research Board (**http://www.ahrb.ac.uk/**), the National Heritage Fund, and more recently the New Opportunities Fund (**http://www.nof-digitise.org**). All of these have been (or currently are) funding digitization projects and initiatives.

The beginnings can be traced back to the work of the early 1990s in the main copyright libraries (notably the British Library, the National Library of Scotland and the Bodleian Library) going hand in hand with Peter Robinson's seminal study *The digitization of primary textual sources* (Robinson, 1993). The British Library began work on its Initiatives for Access project (the title itself is telling), which included the digitization of some of the notable treasures from its collections; the most prominent project was the digitization of the *Beowulf* manuscript, the results of which are now available as a two CD-ROM set. Similarly, at about the same time, the University of Oxford began the digitization of its Celtic and Medieval Manuscripts collection. When one discusses these early projects with the people who worked on them, it is clear that they were truly pioneering days when very little was known about the whole area. Hardware and software had to be tweaked to meet the requirements of the digitizers, cradles and new lighting systems had to be developed, and this was all with the limitations of small hard drives (80–100 Mb) and restricted bandwidth.

Undoubtedly, the UK received its most important boost with the announcement of the Electronic Libraries (or ELib) Programme funded as a result of the Joint Funding Council's Library Review Group report in 1993 under Sir Brian Follett. This initiative, plus the Non-formula Funding of Specialized Research Collections in the Humanities, launched a three-phased series of projects, including content creation and delivery, which led to many digitization projects. As a result the UK can now add to its impressive record in the area such important collaborative projects as: Project BUILDER (Birmingham University's Integrated Library Development and Electronic Resource), available at **http://builder.bham.ac.uk**, which included the digitization of historical journals and university examination papers; and the Internet Library of Early Journals (Universities of Oxford, Leeds, Birmingham and Manchester, see **http://www.bodley.ox.ac.uk/ilej/**), which converted 18th and 19th-century periodicals. ELib has now moved on to a wider model known as the Distributed National Electronic Resource, a major initiative including content acquisition and creation. The country's museums have been offering their collections either online or via CD-ROM for several years now, with notable work being performed by the Ashmolean Museum in Oxford, and the British Museum, the Natural History Museum and the Imperial War Museum in London.

Digitization, though, is a world-wide phenomenon. From the Arnamagnean Institutes in Copenhagen and Reykjavik (**http://www.hum.ku.dk/ami/aminst.html** and **http://www.hum.ku.dk/ami/amproject.html**), which aim to produce a catalogue with links to digital images of their complete collection, to the Bibliothèque National de France (**http://www.bnf.fr/**), with its conversion of over 100,000 visual images and 20 million pages of text, the impact in the European sector is notable (undoubtedly given much impetus by the EU-funded DGXIII Telematics for Libraries Programme). Elsewhere, the Australian Co-Operative Digitization Project (**http://www.nla.gov.au/ferg/**), involved in digitizing newspapers from 1840 to 1845, is but one of a series of major initiatives running in Australasia.

However, as with so many areas of information technology, North America, and in particular the US, has seen some of the most important and wide-reaching projects. The main university players have been Yale, Cornell, California, Harvard, Michigan and Virginia, all of which have been pushing forward ideas in the area of digitization, with considerable support from such benefactors as the Research Libraries Group, the Getty Institute, the Coalition for Networked Information, and the Andrew W Mellon foundation. The Library of Congress, in keeping with the moves adopted by the major European copyright libraries (eg the Bibliothèque Nationale de France and the British Library), has also been funding major initiatives, most notably their American Memory Project and National Digital Library Program (**http://lcweb2.loc.gov/**). More recently we have seen such programmes as AMICO (Art Museum Image Consortium at **http://www. amico.org/**), formed by the Association of Art Museum Directors Educational Foundation, Inc, which will be digitizing 50,000 images, and the continued expansion of the JSTOR service (**http://www.jstor.ac.uk/** and **http://www. jstor.org/**), with its extensive backruns of printed academic journals.

The following then is a highly selective list, but is representative nonetheless of the types of projects that have been initiated. For a continually updated list see UNESCO, IFLA and the British Library's *Directory of Digitized Collections* (**http://thoth.bl.uk/**). Nevertheless, all of these point to projects involved in digitization, ie content creation. Other initiatives and studies (of equal importance) are indicated in Appendix C.

AMICO (Art Museum Image Consortium) (**http://www.amico.org/home. html**). An impressive collaborative venture involving fine art, totalling over 50,000 images.

Arnamagnæan Institutes in Copenhagen and Reykjavik (**http://www.hum.ku. dk/ami/aminst.html** and **http://www.hum.ku.dk/ami/amproject. html**). Aim to produce a catalogue with links to digital images of the complete collection.

Australian Co-operative Digitization Project (**http://www.nla.gov.au/ferg/**). A collaborative scanning project of Australian newspapers from 1840 to 1845.

Biblioteca Telematica Italiana (**http://cibit.humnet.unipi.it**). An electronic text project of Italian literature, see Tavoni and Petrucciani (1999).

Bridgeman Art Library (**http://www.bridgeman.co.uk**). A virtual gallery and image service bringing together collections drawn from over 800 museums and galleries.

British Library (**http://www.bl.uk/**). Details of their Initiatives for Access and the Digital Libraries Programme. Also such material as the Burney Collection at the British Library (**http://minos.bl.uk/diglib/access/microfilm-digitisation.html**) – 1500 reels of early English newspapers from the Civil War onwards. See also the National Library of Scotland (**http://www. nls.uk/**), and the National Library of Wales (**http://www.llgc.org.uk/**).

British Museum (**http://www.thebritishmuseum.ac.uk/compass**). Launched in June 2000, this site presents a searchable index of images taken from the Museum's collections.

BUILDER (Birmingham University's Integrated Library Development and Electronic Resource) (**http://builder.bham.ac.uk**). A major hybrid library project funded under the eLib project aimed at developing 'a working model of the hybrid library within both a teaching and research context, seamlessly integrating information sources, local and remote, using a web-based interface, and in a way which will be universally applicable.'

University of California at Berkeley (**http://www.berkeley.edu**). Has its own digital library and finding aids initiative. See also the California Heritage Collection *Digitizing the collection: image capture* (**http://sunsite.berkeley. edu/CalHeritage/image.html**), which discusses the 1996 project which involved adding images (thumbnails) to finding aids for collections held at the Bancroft Library.

Caribbean Newspapers Imaging Project (**http://www.karamelik.uflib.**

ufl.edu/projects/mellon/). Based at the University of Florida and funded by the Mellon foundation. Used collections at the A Smathers Libraries, digitizing from microfilm 265,000 pages of Caribbean newspapers.

Centre for Retrospective Digitization, Göttingen University Library, Germany (http://www.sub.uni–goettingen.de/gdz/). An initiative involved in retrospective conversion of library materials to build a German Digital Research Library.

Colorado Digitization Project (http://coloradodigital.coalliance.org/toolbox.html). Includes an extremely useful site of links to the major topics surrounding digitization.

CORBIS (http://www.corbis.com/). Billed as the 'place for pictures on the Internet', an extensive online commercially driven image marketplace.

Cornell University (http://www.cornell.edu/). Most notable for the purposes of this report are the Cornell Institute for Digital Collections (http://CIDC.library.cornell.edu/), their Department for Preservation and Conservation (http://www.library.cornell.edu/preservation/) and the Cornell University Prototype Digital Library (http://cdl.library. cornell.edu). Cornell, along with the University of Michigan, was also part of the major Making of America initiative (http://moa.cit.cornell. edu/MOA/), which developed many of the techniques used today.

Council on Library and Information Resources (CLIR) (http://www.clir. org/). Runs four programmes – Commission on Preservation and Access, Digital Libraries, The Economics of Information, and Leadership – and commissions numerous publications. Their Commission on Preservation and Access (http://www.clir.org/programs/cpa/cpa.html) states that 'some information is created digitally and exists only that way, but historical materials are also being digitized as a means of providing access to special collections that have been locked in libraries and archives to prevent their deterioration. All digital files pose serious preservation problems, and finding ways to assure the safekeeping and accessibility of knowledge in this new format is among CLIR's highest priorities.' CLIR also produces *CLIR News*, a regular journal exploring relevant issues.

DEBORA Project (http://www2.echo.lu/libraries/en/projects/debora. html). Although just starting, this EC project aims to 'develop tools for

accessing collections of rare 16th century documents via networks. This
includes the setting up of a production chain for digitizing old books.
Digitization will yield sets of images to be stored and indexed in an Image
Base Management System (IBMS), accessible via the world wide web. The
tools will also incorporate image recognition and features supporting co-
operative work.'

Early English Books Online (EEBO) (**http://wwwlib.umi.com/eebo**). One
of the largest microfilming digitization projects around, aiming to make
digital facsimiles of 125,000 early books in English available via the web.

The Electronic Buddhist Text Initiative (**http://www.human.toyogakuen-u.
ac.jp/~acmuller/ebti.htm**). An international digitization project drawing
together collections from around the world (including the British Library's
Dunhuang collection).

Gettyimages (**http://www.gettyimages.com/**). Another extensive digital
image library available on the web.

Gutenberg Digital Project (**http://www.gutenbergdigital.de/**). An initiative
from the Göttingen State and University Library.

Harvard University (**http://www.harvard.edu**). Harvard has recently launched
its Visual Information Access initiative (**http://via.harvard.edu:748/
html/VIA.html**), which aims to be a 'union catalog of visual resources at
Harvard'.

Hawaiian Newspaper Project (**http://hypatia.slis.hawaii.edu/~hnp/
welcome.html**). This project seeks to make available selected heavily used
Hawaiian-language newspapers (1834–1948) to students throughout the
state of Hawaii who have access to the world wide web (WWW).

Higher Education Digitization Service (HEDS) (**http://heds.herts.ac.uk/**).
Although this is not strictly a digital imaging initiative, it has been
responsible for advising on, and brokering, deals for many digital imaging
projects in the UK. It also holds a good repository of information and
articles. See also the papers posted after the Planning and Implementing a
Digitization Project conference held on 29 June at the British Library
(**http://heds.herts.ac.uk/conf/conf2000.html**).

HELIX (Higher Education Library Image Exchange) (**http://www.helix.
dmu.ac.uk/he_home.htm**). A JISC-funded project under the eLib

initiative to access three collections: the Hulton Getty Collection, the National Art Slide Library and the Valentine Photographic Archive.

IBM Digital Library (**http://www-4.ibm.com/software/is/dig-lib/**). Includes work with the Vatican Library, the Institute for Scientific Information and the Los Angeles Public Library.

JIDI (JISC Image Digitization Initiative) (**http://www.ilrt.bris.ac.uk/jidi/**). A collection of digital imaging projects across UK higher education sector.

Joint Information Systems Committee (JISC) (**http://www.jisc.ac.uk**). The main funding body at higher and further education level in the UK, responsible for initiating a range of digitization initiatives such as JIDI above.

Journal of Electronic Publishing (**http://www.press.umich.edu/jep/**). A good collection of articles published by the University of Michigan Press.

JSTOR (**http://www.jstor.ac.uk** and **http://www.jstor.org/**). Full-text searchable archive of scholarly journals linked to digital facsimiles of the pages.

Library of Congress American Memory Project and National Digital Library Program (**http://lcweb2.loc.gov/**). It is strongly recommended that interested parties look at their *Quality review of document images* internal training guide, which provides a comprehensive discussion of the problems and recommended solutions adopted in the project (**http://lcweb2.loc. gov/ammem/award/docs/docimqr.html**). In addition, in association with Ameritech, the LOC have run a National Digital Library Competition (**http://memory.loc.gov/ammem/award/lessons.html**). This 'lessons learned' briefing covers a range of projects, including:

- the *African-American Experience in Ohio, 1850–1920*
  (**http://memory.loc.gov/ammem/award/97award/ohio.html**)
- *Historic American Sheet Music*
  (**http://memory.loc.gov/ammem/award/97award/duke.html**)
- *African-American Sheet Music*
  (**http://memory.loc.gov/ammem/award/97award/brown.html**)
- *Small Town America: Stereoscopic Views from the Dennis Collection, 1850–1910* (**http://memory.loc.gov/ammem/award/97award/ nypl.html**).

See also their Manuscript Digitization Demonstration Project (**http://
memory.loc.gov/ammem/pictel/index.html**). This contains an
extensive overview of differing formats and resolutions for the capture of
black-and-white, greyscale and colour images from manuscripts (with
samples). The Library was also involved in the extensive Digital Libraries
Initiative, in partnership with the National Science Foundation and others,
which has now reached phase two (**http://www.dli2.nsf.gov**). The first
phase included several projects, some looking at digitization itself (such as
those at the University of California at Berkeley and Stanford, Carnegie
Mellon University and the University of Michigan).

University of Michigan (**http://www.umich.edu**). The Humanities Text
Initiative (HTI) (**http://www.hti.umich.edu/**) forms the umbrella
organization for the university's text and image collections.

National Archives and Records Administration's Electronic Access Project
(**http://www.nara.gov/nara/**), especially their *Guidelines for digitizing
archival materials for electronic access* (**http://www.nara.gov/nara/
vision/eap/eapspec.html**).

National Portrait Gallery (**http://www.npg.org.uk/**).

Public Record Office (**http://www.pro.gov.uk/**). The PRO has established
two digital preservation programmes, EROS (Electronic Records from
Office Systems) for the records created in the office networks being
introduced by government bodies, and NDAD (UK National Digital
Archive of Datasets) (**http://ndad.ulcc.ac.uk**) for structured datasets, such
as survey files and databases, in government departments.

University of Oxford. Various projects have been undertaken at Oxford during the
1990s. These include: Ashmolean Museum (**http://www.ashmol.ox.
ac.uk/**); Beazley Archive (**http://www.beazley.ox.ac.uk**); Bodleian
Broadside Ballads Project (**http://www.bodley.ox.ac.uk/mh/ballads/**);
Celtic and Medieval Manuscripts (**http://image.ox.ac.uk/**); Centre for the
Study of Ancient Documents (**http://www.csad.ox.ac.uk/CSAD/
Images.html**); Internet Library of Early Journals (ILEJ), **http://www.
bodley.ox.ac.uk/ilej/**) – in particular ILEJ's final reports; Refugee Studies
Programme Digital Library Project (**http://www.qeh.ox.ac.uk/rsp/**);
Toyota City Imaging Project (**http://www.bodley.ox.ac.uk/toyota/**

openpage.html); Wilfred Owen Multimedia Digital Archive (**http://info.ox.ac.uk/jtap**) – plus numerous others forthcoming such as an Incunabula project and a pre–1916 manuscript acquisition catalogue. The University also has a specialized unit for integrating digital resources into teaching known as the Humanities Computing Development Team (**http://www.oucs.ox.ac.uk/hcdt**), which has digitized both library and museum collections. Finally, in 1998–9 Oxford University, funded by the A W Mellon foundation, conducted a scoping study into the possible future digitization activities at the university (**http://www.bodley.ox.ac.uk/scoping/**).

Research Libraries Group (RLG), (**http://www.rlg.ac.uk** or **http://www.rlg.org**). The RLG has launched a series of Digital Initiatives (**http://www.rlg.ac.uk/digital/**), publications (including the excellent *RLG DigiNews*) and reports (such as the RLG Working Group on Preservation Issues of Metadata (**http://www.rlg.ac.uk/preserv/presmeta.html**). See Katherine Martinez's concise summary of the RLG's Cultural Heritage Initiatives (**http://www.rlg.ac.uk/digital/spectra.article.html**), and also the new *Guides to quality in visual resource imaging* issued jointly with the Digital Library Federation (**http://www.rlg.ac.uk/visguides**).

The Shetland Museum (**http://www.shetland-museum.org.uk/museum/**). The museum has an internal digital imaging unit converting its extensive photographic collections.

Smithsonian Institute Libraries (**http://www.sil.si.edu/**). See especially the list of sites applicable to preservation issues, traditional and electronic (**http://www.sil.si.edu/Branches/prehp.htm#other**).

Stanford University's Digital Libraries Project (**http://www–diglib.stanford.edu/diglib/index.html/**).

UNESCO's Memory of the World (**http://www.unesco.org/webworld/memory/mempage.htm**). 'The twofold purpose of the UNESCO's 'Memory of the World' programme is to safeguard and promote the endangered world documentary heritage.'

University of Virginia (**http://www.uva.edu**). An important and extensive series of digitization projects housed under the library sector, including the

Electronic Text Centre (**http://etext.lib.virginia.edu/**), the Special
Collections Digital Centre (**http://www.lib.virginia.edu/speccol/scdc/
scdc.html**), and the Institute for Advanced Technology in the Humanities
(**http://jefferson.village.virginia.edu/**). See also their helpful series of
tips for image scanning (**http://etext.lib.virginia.edu/helpsheets/
scanimage.html**).

Yale's Open Book Project (**http://www.library.yale.edu/preservation/
pobweb.html**). Yale University Library's major project to convert 10,000
books from microfilm to digital form, using Xerox Corp for the outsourced
scanning. Reports available at the CLIR sites (**http://www.clir.
org/cpa/reports/openbook/openbook.html** and **http://www.clir.
org/cpa/reports/conway/conway.html**).

Appendix B
Questionnaires

The following questionnaires are aimed at assisting readers who wish to embark on an assessment of their institution's holdings with regard to possible future digitization. These are not unique in their questions, and readers may also wish to look at complementary exercises such as the RLG and NPO's *Survey on preparation*, available at

http://www.thames.rlg.preserv/joint/preparation_survey.html.

Questionnaire 1

To assist in an initial survey of digitization activity at your institution. [This could be used as a means of finding out what activity has already taken place, and what may be on the horizon. Printed copies could be circulated and/or a web form mounted.]

The aims of the questionnaire are:

1   To find out what digitization projects are in progress or have recently been completed, and in so doing to look at existing commitments to maintaining digital projects.
2   To find out what is the potential for digitization by looking at existing archives/collections.

General details

Name:

Unit:

Contact address:

Telephone:

E-mail:

URL:

Is your unit currently involved in, or it has already completed, a digitization project? (Digitization project means the conversion of items from analogue into digital format.)

YES_____ NO _____

If YES please proceed to Section I. If NO go to Section II.

I   Existing digitization project(s) – repeat for each separate project

Please name the project:

Give a brief description of the project (including number and types of items, resulting file sizes etc):

Please give brief details of any articles or websites with further information about the project:

II   Potential digitization projects

Section II is aimed at gathering information on potential digitization projects. If you feel that this is applicable to any collections you are interested in digitizing, then please complete it as appropriate.

Is your unit currently considering any of its collections as possible candidates for digitization?

YES_____ NO _____

If YES please give brief details:

Does your unit have any archives/collections/holdings which you think would be suitable for digitizing?

YES_____ NO _____

If YES please give brief details:

Questionnaire 2

To be used when visiting a proposed collection. This will allow you to gain sufficient information to complete the initial assessment stage (as outlined in Chapter 2). It is recommended that this interview be conducted at the site of the collection.

Name:
Unit:
Contact address:
Contact telephone number:
Contact fax number:
Contact e-mail address:
URL:

1   Does your unit hold any digital materials in its holdings for which it assumes responsibility for their preservation?

YES_____ NO_____

2 Does your unit accept or acquire (through donation, legal deposit or purchase) electronic records for which it assumes preservation responsibility?

YES_____ NO_____

3 Is your unit currently involved in, or has it already completed, a digitization project? (Digitization project means the conversion of items from analog into digital format.)

YES_____ NO_____

The following questions refer to archives and collections which might be considered for digitization:

4 What is the given name of the archive?

5 What is the subject and significance of the archive?

6 What cohesive subgroups does the archive comprise and what numbers do these amount to (eg numbers of journals, books, letters, pages, photographs, posters, postcards, audio cassettes, records, films, videos, etc)?

7 What are the formats and nature of the material (medium, size, b/w v colour, mountings, significant detail, number of colours, handwritten/printed etc)?

8 What is the overall condition of the material contained?

9 Are there any existing non-digital surrogates of the material (eg slides, photographs)? If so, are these of sufficient quality?

10 What documentation and catalogues are available relevant to the archive? Are items uniquely identified and can this be used as the base for file naming?

11 What is the copyright situation? Are you able to confirm the ownership of the rights to copy this material?

12 Are any of the materials yet digitized?

13 Could the physical format of the material tolerate possible digitization processes without risk to its physical form?

14 Would there need to be an intermediary process prior to digital capture to safeguard the item (eg as a result of binding, light-sensitive material, conservation treatment)?

15 Would there need to be special cradles or lighting?

16 Can the material be removed to an external location for digitizing? In particular, can it be moved solely within the institution, or is it permissible to move the material to an external site?

17 Will the physical format allow clear sight of all information with the chosen digitization process (if known)?

18 Do you have any digitization equipment in-house?

19 What resources are available internally to assist in the packaging, preparatory work and handling of the collection?

20 How might this archive relate to other projects or related collections, either within the institution or externally?

21 How is the archive funded?

22 Do you know of any external funding which could be sought to help digitize the collection?

23 What institutional support could be offered for long-term maintenance of the archive?

24 What current needs would the resulting digital archive satisfy (eg preservation, access, both)?

25 How would you envisage the reader using the archive?

26 Any further comments?

Appendix C
Further reading

The following list should be seen as a starting point for people interested in pursuing the area of digital imaging, and accompanies the list of sample initiatives and projects provided in Appendix A. It is clear, though, that certain texts stand out as essential reading for people interested in this area. In particular, Kenney and Reiger (2000) is recommended as providing an excellent next step, covering many of the technical details omitted from this book for reasons of space, and providing numerous real-life case studies of projects. To this one should also add the online publications of TASI, and the *Guides to good practice* issued by the Arts and Humanities Data Service (all of which are noted below). Most recently the RLG and the DLF have launched a series of *Guides to Quality in Visual Resource Imaging* (**http://www.rlg.ac.uk/visguides/**) which include: Colet, L S *Planning a digital imaging project*; Williams, D *Selecting a scanner*; D'Amato, D *Imaging systems: the range of factors affecting image quality*; and Frey, F *Measuring quality of digital masters* and *File formats for digital masters*. To assist in a current awareness strategy, readers should also regularly read such journals as *Ariadne, D-Lib Magazine, International Journal on Digital Libraries, Journal of Digital Information, Journal of Electronic Publishing* and *RLG DigiNews*.

Aquarelle (**http://aqua.inria.fr/**). EC-funded project aimed at validating and demonstrating standards supporting cultural documentation exchange. So far it has produced a Z39.50 application profile; an SGML DTD for producing thematic folders related to architectural assets, an SGML DTD for producing thematic folders related to museum collections and exhibitions, and an SGML DTD for indexing folders.

Ariadne (**http://www.ariadne.ac.uk/**). An excellent online journal that regularly hosts a metadata 'corner' by Charles Oppenheim.

Arms, C (1996) Historical collections for the National Digital Library: lessons and challenges at the Library of Congress, *D-Lib Magazine*, (April) and (May), available at **http://www.dlib.org/dlib/april96/loc/04c-arms.html** and **http://www.dlib.org/dlib/may96/loc/05c-arms.html**. A useful preliminary review of the National Digital Library Program's (NDLP) digitization of Americana at the Library of Congress.

Arms, W (2000) *Digital libraries and electronic publishing*, MIT. Excellent study of the impact of digitization on libraries; and a comprehensive survey of various initiatives, topics and projects.

Arts and Humanities Data Service (**http://www.ahds.ac.uk/**). The main website of the AHDS, with links to all the service providers and numerous invaluable reports. See in particular the *Managing digital collections* section (**http://ahds.ac.uk/manage/manintro.html**), with its series of reports, their *Guides to good practice* (noted above), the report on Digital Preservation (**http://www.ahds.ac.uk/resource/preserve.html**), and their document on *Information Interchange Standards* (**http://www.ahds.ac.uk/resource/standards.html**).

Atkinson, R (1986) Selection for preservation: a materialistic approach, LRTS, 30, 34–62.

Ayris, P (1998) *Guidance for selecting materials for digitisation*, Joint RLG and NPO Preservation, 21–7, available at **http://www.rlg.org/preserv/joint/**.

Beagrie, N and Greenstein, D (1998) *A strategic policy framework for creating and preserving digital collections: a report to the Digital Archiving Working Group*, British Library Research and Innovation Report 107, British Library Research and Innovation Centre, available at **http://ahds.ac.uk/manage/framework.htm**.

Bergamin, G (1999) A standard for the legal deposit of on-line publications. In *The digital library: challenges and solutions for the new millennium*, IFLA, 119–27. Includes a useful summary of the NEDLIB project.

Besser H and Trant, J (1995) *Issues in constructing an image database*, available at **http://www.getty.edu/gri/standard/introimages/index.html**.

Besser, H and Yamashita, R (1998) *The cost of digital image distribution*, available at

http://sunsite.berkeley.edu/Imaging/Databases/1998mellon. An extensive Mellon-funded report of the Museum Education Site License Project (MESL).

Braid, A (1999) Improved access for end users through the use of standards. In *The digital library: challenges and solutions for the new millennium*, IFLA, 97–106. A good synopsis of the Z39.50 and the interlibrary loan (ILL) protocols.

Brisson, R (1998) The world discovers cataloguing, *Journal of Internet cataloguing*, **1** (4). Preprint available at **http://www.personal.psu.edu/faculty/r/o/rob1/publications/JIC metadata**. PDF.

Brown, D S (1999) Image capture beyond 24-Bit RGB, *RLG DigiNews*, **15** (3), available at **http://www.thames.rlg.org/preserv/diginews/diginews3-5.html#technical**

Burnard, L and Sperberg-McQueen, C M (eds) (1994) *Guidelines for electronic text encoding and interchange*, TEI P3 Text Encoding Initiative, Oxford, revised 1999 available at **http://www.hcu.ox.ac.uk/TEI/Guidelines/**.

Caspe, B *How digital cameras work*, Matco Digital Imaging Inc, available at **http://www.cmospro.com/howdcw.htm**. A good overview of the basic terminology.

CEDARS (CURL Exemplars in Digital Archives), available at **http://www.leeds.ac.uk/cedars/**. The leading UK-based project investigating digital preservation. CEDARS have published their outline specifications for 'metadata for digital preservation', which are available on the site.

Chapman, S (1998) *Guidelines for image capture*. In RLG/NPO *Guidelines for digital imaging*, available at **http://www.rlg.ac.uk/preserv/joint/**, 39–60.

Chapman, S, Conway, P and Kenney, A R (1999) Digital imaging and preservation microfilm: the future of the hybrid approach for the preservation of brittle books, *RLG DigiNews*, **3** (1), Febraruy 15, 1999, available at **http://www.thames.rlg.org/preserv/diginews/diginews3-1.html**

Columbia University (1998) *Selection criteria for digital imaging projects*, available at **http://www.Columbia.edu/cu/libraries/digital/criteria.htm**

D-Lib Magazine, available at **http://www.dlib.org**

D'Amato, D and Klopfenstein, R C (1996) Requirements and options for the digitization of the illustration collections of the National Museum of Natural *History*, (March), available at **http://www.nmnh.si.edu/cris/ techrpts/imagopts/index.html**. This comprehensive study of the digitization of fish illustrations for the Museum takes the project through its various stages of selection, benchmarking and digitization.

Day, M (1999) *Metadata for preservation*, CEDARS Project Document AIW01, available at **http://www.ukoln.ac.uk/metadata/cedars/AIW01.html**

Day, M (1999) *Issues and approaches to preservation metadata*, Joint RLG and NPO Preservation, available at **http://www.rlg.org/preserv/joint/**, 73–84.

Day, M (1997) Extending metadata for digital preservation, *Ariadne,* **9**, **http://www.ariadne.ac.uk/issue9/metadata/intro.html**

Digital Heritage and Cultural Content (**http://www.echo.lu/digicult/en/ backgrd.html**). EC-funded site looking at libraries and technology. Includes the full copy of *Digitization of library materials*, report of the concentration meeting and workshop held in Luxembourg, 14 December 1998.

Dovey, M (1999) Meta-objects: an object oriented approach to metadata, *Ariadne,* **19**, **http://www.ariadne.ac.uk/issue19/meta–objects/**

Dublin Core (**http://purl.oclc.org/dc/**). In addition to this home page for the initiative, one should also consult UKOLN's online utility to help in creating Dublin Core metadata (**http://www.ukoln.ac.uk/metadata/dcdot/**).

EAD Tag Library (**http://lcweb.loc.gov/ead/tglib/tlhome.html**). A comprehensive study of the EAD tag sets.

Edens, J (2000) *Resources for digitization* (**http://ublib.buffalo.edu/libraries/ units/cts/preservation/digires.html**). An extremely useful list of web resources covering many of the topics discussed in this book.

Fresko, M and Tombs, K (1999) *Digital Preservation Guidelines*, European Commission, DG XIII/E, available at **http://www.echo.lu/digicult/en/ backgrd.html**

Frey, F (1997) Digital imaging for photographic collections: foundations for technical standards, *RLG DigiNews*, **1** (3), December 15, 1997 (**http://www.rlg.org/preserv/diginews/diginews3.html#com**).

Frey, F S and Reilly, J M (1999) *Digital imaging for photographic collections: foundations for technical standards*, report sponsored by the NEH, available at **http://www.rit.edu/ipi**

Gertz, J (1999) *Guidelines for digital imaging*, RLG/NPO, available at **http://www.rlg.ac.uk/preserv/joint/**, 11–19.

Global Inventory Project (**http://www.gip.int**). An EC and G8-funded project that allows one to search an inventory of digital initiatives. Described as a 'one-stop facility' linking distributed national and international inventories of projects, studies and other activities relevant to the promotion and the further development of knowledge and understanding of the Information Society.

Gould, S and Ebdon, R (1999) *IFLA/UNESCO Survey on Digitization and Preservation*, IFLA.

Granger, S, Harmsen, L and Hemsley, J R (1996) *Selected Technology Issues*, MAGNETS, available at **http://www.vasari.co.uk/magnets/wp5/**. A Museum and Galleries New Technology Study (MAGNETS) as part of the Telematics Application Programme Administrations Sector Project AD1101 that gives a good overview (though a bit outdated now) of digitization.

Greenstein, D (2000) The challenge of preservation in creating digital library services, *CLIR News*, **15** (May/June), available at **http://www.clir.org/pubs/issues/issue15.html**

Hazen, D, Horrell, J and Merill-Oldham, J (1998) *Selecting research collections for digitization*, Council on Library and Information Resources; European Commission of Preservation and Access.

Heinink, L (1999) *Copyright*, Oxford, available at **http://www.bodley.ox.ac.uk/scoping/appi.html**. A report on UK Copyright for Oxford University's Scoping Study on Digitization.

Hendley, T (1997) *Comparison of methods and costs of digital preservation*, British Library Research and Innovation Report 106, British Library Research and Innovation Centre, available at **http://www.ukoln.ac.uk/services/elib/papers/tavistock/hendley/hendley.html**

Howell, A (1997) Film scanning of newspaper collections: international initiatives, *RLG DigiNews*, **1** (2), available at **http://www.thames.rlg.org/preserv/diginews/diginews2.html#film-scanning**. A useful review of three initiatives: the Burney Collection at the BL, the Caribbean Newspaper Imaging Project at the University of Florida, and the Australian Co-Operative Digitization Project. Outlines the problems and opportunities of scanning newspapers (all from microfilm).

Ianella, R (1997) The resource discovery project, *Ariadne*, **8** (**http://www. ariadne.ac.uk/issue8/resource-discovery/intro.html**). An overview of the RDP initiative in Australia.

IFLA (International Federation of Library Associations) *Digital libraries metadata resources* (**http://www.nlc-bnc.ca/ifla/II/metadata.htm**). Includes discussions of Dublin Core, the Warwick Framework, and RDF. See also *The definition and purposes of a digital library* (1995), available at **http://www.ifla.org/documents/libraries/net/arl-dlib.txt**

INDECS (**http://www.indecs.org/**). Interoperability of e-commerce systems – concerned with applying metadata to rights of reproduction.

Initiatives in Digital Information (**http://www.lib.umich.edu/libhome/ IDINews/**).

International Colour Consortium (**http://www.color.org**). An in-depth look at colour management systems and their history.

International Committee for Documentation of the International Council of Museums (ICOM-CIDOC) (**http://www.cidoc.icom.org/cidoc0. htm**) have produced (jointly) with the Getty Information Institute the papers *Developments in museum and cultural heritage information standard* (**http://www.cidoc.icom.org/stand1.htm**) and *Museum and cultural heritage information standards resource guide* (**http://www.cidoc.icom.org/ stand2.htm**).

International Journal on Digital Libraries (**http://link.springer.de/link/ service/journals/00799/**).

Journal of Digital Information (**http://jodi.ecs.soton.ac.uk/**).

Journal of Electronic Publishing (**http://www.press.umich.edu/jep/**).

Journal of Internet Cataloguing (**http://jic.libraries.psu.edu/**). The Internet site of this printed journal contains full-text versions of back-issues and occasional links to pre-print articles.

Keene, S (last updated 2000) *Museums and the information age* (**http://www.s-keene.dircon.co.uk/infoage/**).

Kenney, A (1996) *Digital to microfilm conversion: a demonstration project 1994-96*, NEH Report, available at **http://www.cornell.library.edu/ preservation/ pub.htm**

Kenney, A (1997) The Cornell Digital Microfilm Conversion Report: final project to NEH, *RLG DigiNews*, **1** (2), available at **http://www.thames.rlg.org/ preserv/diginews/diginews2.html#com**. A summary report of the Computer Output Microfilm project involving 177 reels of 19th and 20th-century agricultural history documents.

Kenney, A and Chapman, S (1996a) Digital conversion of research library materials: a case for full informational capture, *D-Lib Magazine*, available at **http://www.dlib.org/dlib/october96/cornell/10chapman.html**

Kenney, A and Chapman, S (1996b) *Digital imaging for libraries and archives*, Cornell University Library. Commonly known as the 'red book' this accompanied a series of workshops in the US. An invaluable guide full of very useful material, especially the early discussions of basic terminology, and Chapter Seven ('Film Scanning').

Kenney, A R and Rieger, O Y (1998) *Managing digital imaging projects: an RLG workshop*, RLG. This has become known as the 'white book' – again an invaluable book tackling many management issues.

Kenney, A and Rieger, O (eds) (2000) *Moving theory into practice: digital imaging for libraries and archives*, RLG.

Klemperer, K and Chapman, S (1997) Digital libraries: a selected resource guide, *Information Technology and Libraries*, **16** (3), available at **http://www.lita.org/ ital/1603_klemperer.htm**

Klijn, E and de Ludenet, Y (2000) *In the picture: preservation and digitisation of European photographic collections*, European Commission. A good survey of many European projects, including the results of an interesting survey of photographic archives.

Kodak Image Products *Glossary of Imaging Terms* (**http://www.kofax.com/ Support/ts_glossary.htm**). A handy reference list of key terminology in digitization.

Kunze, J *Encoding Dublin Core metadata in HTML* (1999) (**http://www.ietf.org/ internet-drafts/draft-kunze-dchtml-00.txt**).

Lee, S D and Groves, P (1999) *On-Line tutorials and digital archives or 'digitising Wilfred'* (**http://www.jtap.ac.uk**). Full report on the Wilfred Owen Multimedia Digital Archive, including digitization costs.

Leggate, P (1997) *Internet Library of Early Journals annual report*, ILEJ, available at

http://www.bodley.ox.ac.uk/ilej/papers/ar1997.htm. A good overview of an individual project and some of the issues that were involved.

Library of Congress *Step-by-step instructions* (**http://lcweb2.loc.gov/ammemm/award/docs/docimqr.html**). A guide to the quality review process used for the American Memory Project.

LIC (1997) *Virtually new: creating the digital collection: a review of digitisation projects in local authority libraries and archives*. A report to the Library and Information Commission prepared by Information North (**http://www.lic.gov.uk/publications/virtually/index.html**)

McIntyre, J E (1998) Protecting the physical form, RLG/NPO *Guidelines for Digital Imaging*, **http://www.rlg.ac.uk/preserv/joint/**, pp. 33-8.

Micham, L and Faulds, D (1999) Making British heritage available on the world wide web: the state of digitization in special collections librarianship in Great Britain, *Journal of the Association for History and Computing*, **2** (3), available at **http://mcel.pacificu.edu/jahc/jahcII3/ARTICLESII3/Heritage/heritage.html**

Miller, B I (2000) Recent lessons from the courts: the changing landscape of copyright, *RLG DigiNews*, **4** (2), available at **http://www.rlg.ac.uk/preserv/diginews/**

Miller, P (1996) Metadata for the masses, *Ariadne*, **5** (**http://www.ariadne.ac.uk/issue5/metadata-masses/intro.html**). Predominantly concentrating on Dublin Core issues.

Moore, R, et al (2000) Collection-based persistent digital archives (part 1), *D-Lib Magazine*, **6** (3), available at **http://www.dlib.org/dlib/march00/moore/03moore-pt1.html**

Morrison, A, Popham, M and Wikander, K (2000) *Creating and documenting electronic texts: a guide to good practice*, available at **http://ota.ahds.ac.uk/documents/creating/**

National Preservation Office (under the British Library Site at **http://www.bl.uk/**). They have an explicit digital remit, and are working closely with the CEDARS project.

Netherlands' NEDLIB initiative (**http://www.konbib.nl/nedlib/**).

Noerr, P (1998) *The digital library toolkit*, available at **http://www.sun.com/edu/libraries/digitaltoolkit.html**

Oppenheim, C (1999) JISC Publishers' Association work on developing guidelines for copyright issues in the electronic environment. In *The digital library: challenges and solutions for the new millennium*, IFLA, 39–43.

PADI Project – the National Library of Australia's Preserving Access to Digital Information Project (**http://www.nla.gov.au/padi/**).

Paskin, N (1998) *The digital object identifier system* (talk online **http://www.doi.org/ workshop/minutes/MAY20/sld002.htm**).

Puglia, S (1999) The costs of digital imaging projects, *RLG DigiNews*, **3** (5).

Resource Description Framework (**http://www.w3.org/RDF/**). This W3C initiative promises much for the location of online resources.

RLG (1996) *Preserving digital information: final report and recommendations of the RLG Taskforce*, available at **http://www.rlg.org/ArchTF/**

RLG DigiNews (**http://www.rlg.org/preserv/diginews**). One of the most important journals (online and free) for focusing on digitization issues.

RLG (1998) *Key components to quality guidelines*, report of the RLG Working Group on Digital Image Capture, 1998, available at **http://www.rlg.org/ preserv/ joint/selection.html**

RLG (1999) *Selection criteria, guidelines, decision-making aids*, report of the RLG Working Group on Selection, 1998, available at **http://www.rlg.org/ preserv/ joint/selection.html**

RLG Working Group on Preservation Issues of Metadata (1998) *Final report*, Mountain View (**http://www.rlg.org/preserv/presmeta.html**)

RLG/NPO (1999) *Guidelines for digital imaging*, NPO (**http://www.rlg.ac.uk/ preserv/joint/**). An exemplary collection of papers given at the Joint National Preservation Office and Research Libraries Group Preservation Conference in Warwick, 1998. Many of the papers from this volume are referenced elsewhere in this book.

Robinson, P (1993) *The digitization of primary textual sources*, Oxford.

Rosenblatt, W (1997) Solving the dilemma of copyright protection online: the digital object identifier, *Journal of Electronic Publishing*, **3** (2), available at **http://www.press.umich.edu/jep/03-02/doi.html**

Smith, A (1999) *Why digitize?* and *The future of the past: preservation in American research libraries*, CLIR, available at **http://www.clir.org/pubs/reports/**

reports.html. New reports at the CLIR site. Both studies come down heavily on the side of digitization for access as opposed to preservation.

Swartzel, A G (1998) Preparation of materials for digitization. In RLG/NPO *Guidelines for Digital Imaging*, **http://www.rlg.ac.uk/preserv/joint/**, 29–32.

Swora, T (1996) *Selecting library and archive collections for digital reformatting*, Mountain View.

Tanner, S (2000) From vision to implementation: strategic and management issues for digital collections, paper presented at The Electronic Library seminar, February 2000. See the HEDS site (**http://heds.herts.ac.uk/**).

Tanner, S and Lomax, J (1999a) *Digitisation: How much does it really cost?*, paper presented to the Digital Resources for the Humanities Conference, King's College, London, September 1999). See the HEDS site (**http://heds.herts. ac.uk/**).

Tanner, S and Lomax, J (1999b) *Future technologies for preserving the past: creating digital image collection content*, paper presented at the workshop Scanning and Recognition Technology, University of Herfordshire, June 1999. See the HEDS site (**http://heds.herts.ac.uk/**).

TASI (Technical Advisory Service for Images) *Creating digital image archives* (**http://www.tasi.ac.uk/**). An extensive repository of documents giving overviews on all areas of digital imaging, including image quality and colour management issues and JIDI image quality assurance.

Tavoni, M and Petrucciani, A (1999) 'The Italian Digital Library Project (Biblioteca Telematica Italiana, *The digital library: challenges and solutions for the new millennium*, IFLA, 87–93.

TEI and XML in digital libraries (**http://www.hti.umich.edu/misc/ssp/ workshops/teidlf/sumrec.html**). A report on a two-day workshop held in 1998 and hosted by the Library of Congress.

UKOLN *Metadata site* (**http://www.ukoln.ac.uk/metadata/**). UKOLN has been actively investigating the area of electronic metadata for some time now. It is involved in several projects, all of which are worth following up.

Virtual Heritage Network (**http://www.virtualheritage.net**). A good site for news and articles.

Webb, C (1996) *The Ferguson Project: a hybrid approach to reformatting rare*

Australiana, available at **http://www.nla.gov.au/nla/staffpaper/cwebb1. html**. A National Library of Australia project based on John Alexander Ferguson's *Bibliography of Australia*. Outlines the benefits of the hybrid approach (microfilm and digitization).

Wendler, R (1999) *Metadata in the library*, Harvard University Library, (**http://hul.harvard.edu/ldi/html/metadata.html**).

Williams, J (1998) Guidelines for image capture: a UK perspective. In RLG/NPO *Guidelines for digital imaging*, available at (**http://www.rlg.ac. uk/preserv/joint/**), 61–71.

Index